…ehensive Guide For The New Muslim

Important lessons to help the new Muslim correctly practice Islam

Prepared by Anwar Wright
A graduate of the Islamic University of Madinah, the College of Hadīth Studies

First Edition: 1439H/August 2018CE

Author: Anwar Wright
Reviewed and Edited: Ḥikmah Publications
Ḥikmah Publications
ISBN: 978-1-5323-6937-7

Address:
Ḥikmah Publications
P.O. Box 44121
Philadelphia, PA. 19144
hikmahpubs@gmail.com

Transliteration Table

Consonants

ء	ʾ	د	d	ض	ḍ	ك	k
ب	b	ذ	dh	ط	ṭ	ل	l
ت	t	ر	r	ظ	ẓ	م	m
ث	th	ز	z	ع	ʿ	ن	n
ج	j	س	s	غ	gh	ه	h
ح	ḥ	ش	sh	ف	f	و	w
خ	kh	ص	ṣ	ق	q	ي	y

Vowels

Short	ـَ	a	ـِ	i	ـُ	u
Long	ـَا	ā	ـِي	ī	ـُو	ū

Diphthongs	ـَوْ	aw	ـَيْ	ay

عَزَّوَجَلَّ	The Mighty and Majestic.
سُبْحَانَهُ وَتَعَالَىٰ	The Sublime and Exalted.
صَلَّى ٱللَّهُ عَلَيْهِ وَسَلَّمَ	May Allāh make good mention of His Prophet in the highest company and grant him safety in this life and the next.
رَضِيَ ٱللَّهُ عَنْهُ	May Allāh be pleased with him.
رَحِمَهُ ٱللَّهُ	May Allāh show mercy to him.
عَلَيْهِ ٱلسَّلَامُ	Peace be upon him.

Table of Contents

Foreword
What Is Incumbent Upon the New Muslim To Implement and to Abandon

The Noble Scholar, al-ʿAllāmah
Ṣāliḥ Ibn Fawzān al-Fawzān[1]

All praise is for Allāh and may peace and salutations be upon our Prophet Muḥammad and upon his Family and his Companions. To proceed:

Indeed, Allāh has created the creation for His worship. Allāh said,

﴿ وَمَا خَلَقْتُ ٱلْجِنَّ وَٱلْإِنسَ إِلَّا لِيَعْبُدُونِ ﴿٥٦﴾ ﴾

"And I did not create the Jinn and mankind except to worship Me." [*Sūrah al-Dhāriyāt* 51:56]

Allāh is not to be worshipped, except by that which He has legislated. And He sent His Messengers to clarify to the people whatever He has legislated, because worshipping Allāh with other than what He has legislated is null and void. And He ended the Messengers with His Messenger: Muḥammad (ﷺ) and He made it obligatory upon all of mankind to follow him.

Allāh the Exalted said,

[1] Taken from http://www.alfawzan.af.org.sa/node/13814. Translation by Maaz Qureshi.

﴿ قُلۡ يَـٰٓأَيُّهَا ٱلنَّاسُ إِنِّي رَسُولُ ٱللَّهِ إِلَيۡكُمۡ جَمِيعًا ﴾

"Say: (O Muḥammad**) O mankind, indeed I am the Messenger of Allāh to you all."** [*Sūrah al-A'rāf* 7:158]

So whoever does not believe in Muḥammad (ﷺ), then he is a disbeliever. The Religion of Muḥammad (ﷺ) is Islām and Allāh will never accept any other religion besides it. Allāh, the Exalted said,

﴿ وَمَن يَبۡتَغِ غَيۡرَ ٱلۡإِسۡلَـٰمِ دِينٗا فَلَن يُقۡبَلَ مِنۡهُ وَهُوَ فِي ٱلۡأٓخِرَةِ مِنَ ٱلۡخَـٰسِرِينَ ٨٥ ﴾

"And whosoever seeks a religion other than Islām, then it will never be accepted of him, and in the Hereafter he will be one of the losers." [*Sūrah Āli-'Imrān* 3:85]

The Islām that Muḥammad (ﷺ) came with has five pillars: **[i]** The testimony that there is none worthy of worship besides Allāh and that Muḥammad is the Messenger of Allāh; **[ii]** The establishment of the Prayer; **[iii]** Payment of the *zakāt* (alms); **[iv]** Fasting in the month of *Ramaḍān*; **[v]** *Ḥajj* (pilgrimage) to the Sacred House of Allāh in accordance with one's ability.[1]

---

[1] **Translator's Note:** From Abī 'Abd al-Raḥmān 'Abdullāh Ibn 'Umar Ibn al-Khaṭṭāb (رَضِيَ ٱللَّهُ عَنْهُمَا) who said, 'I heard the Messenger of Allāh (ﷺ) saying, 'Islām is built upon five: the testimony that there is none worthy of worship besides Allāh and that Muḥammad is the Messenger of Allāh, the establishment of the Prayer, payment of the *zakāt* (alms), *Ḥajj* (pilgrimage) to the House and

What the Individual Who Wishes to Enter into Islām Must Do:

He must utter the two testimonies of faith and then he must offer the pillars of Islām in the following manner:

He must say, "I bear witness that there is none worthy of worship besides Allāh and I bear witness that Muḥammad is the Messenger of Allāh."

أَشْهَدُ أَنْ لا إِلَه إِلا اللهُ وَ أَشْهَدُ أَنَّ مُحَمَّدً رَسُول الله

"*Ash-hadu an lā ilāha illallāh, wa ash-hadu anna Muḥammadan Rasūl Allāh.*" And he must utter this out loud.

He must pray the five Prayers: *al-Fajr* (morning Prayer), *al-Ẓuhr* (noon Prayer), *al-'Aṣr* (afternoon Prayer), *al-Maghrib* (evening Prayer) and *al-'Ishā* (night Prayer) during every day and night throughout the whole of his life.

The *Fajr* Prayer is two units, the *Ẓuhr* Prayer is four units, the *'Aṣr* Prayer is four units, the *Maghrib* Prayer is three units and the *'Ishā* Prayer is four units. And one must not pray, except after he performs the ablution (*wuḍū'*).

That occurs by washing the entirety of the face and washing the hands and arms up to (and including) the elbows and wiping the head and washing the feet up to (and including) the ankles with water that is pure.

---

fasting in the month of *Ramaḍān.*" Related by al-Bukhārī (1/8) and Muslim (16/151).

If he possesses an abundance of wealth, exceeding that for which he has need, he must take out 2.5% of it as *zakāt* (alms) for the needy and the destitute every year. And if his wealth does not exceed his need, then there is no *zakāt* due upon him.

He must fast the month of *Ramaḍān*, and it is the ninth month of the *Hijrī* year. He must abandon eating, drinking and sexual intercourse with his wife from sunrise[1] to sunset. He is permitted to eat, drink and have sexual intercourse with his wife at night only.

If he has the financial and physical capability, then he must perform the *Ḥajj* (pilgrimage) to the House of Allāh at least once in a lifetime. And if he has the financial capability, but he does not have the physical capability due to old age or a chronic illness, then he must entrust someone to perform the *Ḥajj* on his behalf once.

He must perform whatever remains from acts of obedience, since that is a completion of these pillars.

---

[1] **[AW]** Perhaps what the *Shaykh* intended is from dawn to sunset. This is what is established in the *Qur'ān* and *Sunnah*, and also what the *Shaykh* has affirmed in his other works, such as *al-Mulakhkhas al-Fiqhī*.

What Is Incumbent Upon the New Muslim to Abandon:

He must abandon *Shirk* (associating others with Allāh in worship) with all of its types, and it is to worship other than Allāh. And from it is supplication (*du'ā'*) to the dead, sacrificing for them and taking oaths by them.

He must abandon *bida'* (innovations), and they are acts of worship that have not been legislated by the Messenger of Allāh, Muḥammad (صَلَّىٰ ٱللَّٰهُ عَلَيْهِ وَسَلَّمَ), due to the statement of the Prophet (صَلَّىٰ ٱللَّٰهُ عَلَيْهِ وَسَلَّمَ), "Whosoever does an act that is not in accordance with this affair of ours, then it is rejected."[1] That means: it is not accepted.

He must abandon usury (*ribā*), gambling, bribes and lying in dealings and buying and selling unlawful commodities.

He must abandon *zinā* (adultery, fornication). And it is to have sexual intercourse with someone other than his lawfully wedded wife. And he must abandon homosexuality.

He must abandon the consumption of intoxicants, eating swine, whatever was sacrificed for other than Allāh, and eating the dead animals [that died without being slaughtered in a manner permitted in the Islāmic legislation].

He must abandon marriage to the disbelieving women who are not from the people of the Book (i.e. Jews and Christians).

---

[1] Related by Muslim (no. 1718).

He must separate from his disbelieving wife who is not from the people of the Book, except if the disbelieving woman accepts Islām along with him or during her *'iddah*.[1]

If circumcision will not harm him, then he must be circumcised by a Muslim surgeon.

If he is able to move from the land of the disbelievers to the land of Islām, then he must do so. If he is unable, then he must remain in his country and hold onto his Religion.

Written by,
Ṣāliḥ Ibn Fawzān al-Fawzān
Member of the Committee of Major Scholars
19/03/1433H

---

[1] **Translator's Note:** The *'iddah* is the period a woman must observe after the death of her spouse or after a divorce, during which she may not marry another man. Refer to *Majmū'ah As'ilah Tuhimm al-Usrah al-Muslimah* (p. 61-62) of Imām Muḥammad Ibn Ṣāliḥ al-'Uthaymīn (d.1421H).

Chapter One
Actions Are Judged by Intentions

The Prophet (صَلَّىٰ ٱللَّهُ عَلَيْهِ وَعَلَىٰ آلِهِ وَسَلَّمَ) said:

> "Actions are by intentions and a person will only get what they intended. So whoever's migration is for Allāh and His Messenger, then his migration is for Allāh and His messenger. And whoever's migration is to gain something of the worldly life or to marry a woman, then his migration is for what he migrated for.[1]"

Dear Muslim, many of the scholars of Islām would begin their books with this tremendous *ḥadīth*. Although there are many benefits that are derived from this *ḥadīth*, one of the most important is that a person corrects their intention in every action that they do.

Ibn Rajab (رَحِمَهُ ٱللَّهُ) stated about the aforementioned *ḥadīth,*

> "The scholars agree regarding its authenticity and they have received it with full acceptance. Imām Bukhārī began his book '*Ṣaḥīḥ*' with it, and put it in place as an introduction to it. This was a subtle indication from him that every action in which a person does not seek the Face of Allāh, then it is void and has no benefit in this life or the next."[2]

Therefore, every act of worship you do, whether that be learning your religion to draw closer to your Lord, prayer, fasting, or other

[1] Reported by al-Bukhārī and Muslim.
[2] *Jāmiʿ al-ʿUlūm wa al-Ḥikam* (1/61).

than that, then make your intention solely and sincerely for His sake alone, seeking to obtain the great reward He prepared for the believers in the Hereafter.

Chapter Two
The Obligation of Seeking Knowledge

The Messenger of Allāh (صَلَّى ٱللَّٰهُ عَلَيْهِ وَعَلَىٰ آلِهِ وَسَلَّمَ) said:

> "Seeking Knowledge is obligatory upon every Muslim[1]."

Sufyān al Thawrī (رَحِمَهُ ٱللَّٰهُ) said:

> "It is that (knowledge) which the servant has no excuse to be ignorant of."

Shaykh Bin Bāz (رَحِمَهُ ٱللَّٰهُ) said:

> "You, O servant of Allāh, were created for the worship (of Allāh), and have been commanded to perform it in its proper manner in which Allāh legislated. There is no way to obtain this except by (the aid) of Allāh, and then by seeking understanding in the religion. So it is upon everyone Islāmically accountable (for their actions) to learn those matters that are not permissible to be ignorant of, and this goes for men and women. This is so they may learn what is obligatory upon them and what Allāh made impermissible for them, and so that they can perform what Allāh made obligatory upon them, (doing that) upon correctness and insight. And so that one can stay away from what Allāh made prohibited them from, (doing that) upon insight. This is what is obligatory upon everyone[2]."

---

[1] Collected by Ibn Mājah in his *Sunan* (no. 224) and declared *Ṣaḥīḥ Li Ghayrihi* by Shaykh al-Albānī in his book, *Takhrīj Mushkilah al Faqr* (no. 86).

[2] *Waṣāyā li Ṭullāb al-ʿIlm* (p. 17) by way of *Sharḥ Qawl Ibn Sīrīn* (p. 93).

Shaykh Ṣāliḥ al Fawzān said:

> "Among (the types of) knowledge is that which is an individual obligation upon every Muslim to know, and no one is excused of being ignorant of; this is to have knowledge of the matters which the servant's religion cannot be correct except by (learning) them, such as the matters of his *'Aqīdah* (i.e. belief), the rulings of his *Ṣalāh* (i.e. prayer), his giving of *Zakāt* (i.e obligatory charity), his *Ṣawm* (i.e. fasting), and his *Ḥajj* (pilgrimage). Therefore, this area of knowledge - or this portion of knowledge - is obligatory upon every Muslim to know thoroughly, and no one is excused from having ignorance of it. This is because it is not possible that a person's religion be correct except with it."[1]

[1] *Muḥāḍarāt fī al-'Aqīdah wa al-Da'wah* (2/235) by way of the book, *Sharḥ Qawl Ibn Sīrīn* (p. 93).

Chapter Three
The Importance of the Correct ʿAqīdah [Belief]

Know, O Muslim, that the first matter you must give importance to is learning the correct *ʿAqīdah*, or the correct Islāmic belief system. At the head of the *ʿAqīdah* are the matters of *Tawḥīd* and the pillars of *Īmān* (belief), which will be discussed in the next two chapters. *Shaykh* Ṣāliḥ al Fawzān says addressing this important matter:

> "I advise the youth and other than them from the Muslims to give great concern to the *ʿAqīdah* firstly before everything. This is because the *ʿAqīdah* is the foundation which all actions are built upon as far as them being accepted or rejected. If the *ʿAqīdah* is sound and correct and in accordance to what the Messengers came with, especially the seal of them – Muḥammad (صَلَّى ٱللَّهُ عَلَيْهِ وَسَلَّمَ)- then the rest of the actions will be accepted, if they are done sincerely seeking the Face of Allāh the Most High, and in accordance to what Allāh and His Messenger have legislated. However, if the *ʿAqīdah* is corrupted or is misguided due to it being based upon traditions or blind following of one's forefathers, or it is an *ʿAqīdah* that entails *shirk* (associating partners with Allāh), then those actions will be rejected; none of them will be accepted, even if one had done them with sincerity and seeking the Face of Allāh. This is because Allāh does not accept any actions except what is done sincerely seeking His Noble Face, and likewise done upon the *Sunnah* of His messenger (صَلَّى ٱللَّهُ عَلَيْهِ وَسَلَّمَ). So whoever desires salvation for their soul and they desire to have their deeds accepted, and they desire to be a true Muslim,

> then one must give importance to the 'Aqīdah. This is by knowing the sound and correct belief and also knowing what nullifies it and contradicts it, so one can base their actions upon it. This can only occur by learning it from the people of knowledge and the people who have insight who have learned it from the *Salaf*[1] of this *Ummah*. Allāh said to His Prophet (صَلَّى ٱللَّهُ عَلَيْهِ وَسَلَّمَ):
>
> ﴿ فَٱعْلَمْ أَنَّهُۥ لَآ إِلَٰهَ إِلَّا ٱللَّهُ وَٱسْتَغْفِرْ لِذَنۢبِكَ ﴾
>
> **"Know that none has the right to be worshipped except Allāh, then seek forgiveness for your sins."** [Sūrah Muḥammad 47:19]
>
> *Imām* al-Bukhārī (رَحِمَهُ ٱللَّهُ) placed a chapter heading (in his book): "Chapter- Knowledge precedes speech and action." Then he mentioned the previous verse...[2]"

The [Islamic] belief to the other fields of knowledge and actions is equivalent to the foundation of a building and the roots of a tree. So just as the building will not stand except on a foundation, and the tree will not stand except upon its roots, then similarly the actions of an individual and his knowledge will not benefit unless it is built upon the correct belief.

Focusing on matters of belief has precedence over other affairs such as food, drink and clothing because it is through the [correct] belief that the believer lives a truly [happy] life, his soul becomes pure, his

---

[1] We will discuss who the *Salaf* [the pious predecessors] were in an upcoming chapter.

[2] *Al-Ajwibah al-Mufīdah* (p. 91-92).

actions are correct, his acts of obedience are accepted, and he is raised in degrees before Allāh, the Mighty and Majestic.

However, if the belief is faulty, corrupt or absent, then this will have the opposite effect upon all of his affairs and all of his actions. Therefore, a corrupt belief is a source of ruin for the individual as it pertains to his actions and mannerism; and it debases and destroys him.

Shaykh al-Islām Ibn Taymīyah (رَحِمَهُ ٱللَّهُ) said:

> "Additionally, those who oppose *Ahl al-Ḥadīth* [The People Of *Ḥadīth*] are expected to have corrupt actions, either due to an evil belief, hypocrisy, a sickness in the heart or a weakness of faith.
>
> The abandonment of the obligations, transgression of the legislated boundaries, disdain for the [ordained] rights and hardness of the heart is found among them, which is visible to everyone. Many of their Shuyūkh are accused of serious offences."[1]

If the belief is sound and firm, and based upon the Book of Allāh and the *Sunnah* of His Messenger, then the person will be upright because the basis of piety and uprightness is present within him, as Allāh, the Mighty and Majestic said:

﴿ أَلَمْ تَرَ كَيْفَ ضَرَبَ ٱللَّهُ مَثَلًا كَلِمَةً طَيِّبَةً كَشَجَرَةٍ طَيِّبَةٍ أَصْلُهَا ثَابِتٌ وَفَرْعُهَا فِى ٱلسَّمَآءِ ﴿٢٤﴾ ﴾

---

[1] *Naqḍ al-Manṭiq*, p. 45.

> "See you not how Allāh sets forth a parable? - A goodly word as a goodly tree, whose root is firmly fixed, and its branches (reach) to the sky (i.e. very high)." [Ibrahīm: 24]

He (سُبۡحَانَهُۥ وَتَعَالَىٰ) has made the fundamental matters of faith and its foundations – which is belief – equivalent to the roots that the tree stands upon. Thus, if the root is firm, then this tree is closer to completeness in terms of its growth, development and the deliciousness of its fruits, depending upon the correctness of this foundation.[1]

Shaykh al-Islām Ibn Taymīyah (رَحِمَهُ ٱللَّهُ) said:

> "As for *Ahl al-Sunnah wa al-Ḥadīth*, then it is not known that any of their scholars nor righteous common-folk ever renounced their doctrine and creed. Rather, they were the most patient of the people upon that, even if they were tested with all types of tests and trialed with all types of tribulations." *Naqḍ al-Manṭiq*, p. 42.

Compare this with the wavering of the people of theological rhetoric.

Ibn Taymīyah (رَحِمَهُ ٱللَّهُ) said:

> "*Ahl al-Kalām* (those who base their religion upon theological rhetoric) are the people who waver most from one doctrine to another. They [are found] to be certain [about a matter] in one place and then certain about its exact opposite in another place, and they declare the one who asserts this to be a

---

[1] *Sharḥ ʿAqīdah ʿAbd al-Ghanī al-Maqdisī* of Shaykh ʿAbd al-Razzāq al-Badr, p. 8-9.

disbeliever. This is a proof of their lack of certainty." *Majmū' al-Fatāwá* (4/50).

Chapter Four
Tawḥīd and its Types

Dear Muslim, the first obligation upon you is to know Allāh through His *Tawḥīd.* This term *Tawḥīd,* as it relates to the aspect of the Arabic language, means to make something one. As it relates to the religion of Islām, *Tawḥīd* means to single Allāh out with all acts of worship.

Tawḥīd is of three types.

1. *Tawḥīd al-Rubūbiyyah* or *Tawḥīd* of Allāh's Lordship. This means to have belief that Allāh is the sole Creator of everything and that He controls and disposes of all affairs in the heavens and earth and all that is in between them. One can also say that it is to single Allāh out in His actions, such as that He is the sole Creator of all of mankind, the sole Provider of all of mankind, the only One who gives life and causes death, and other than that from His actions. He has no partners in any of that.

Affirming this type of *Tawḥīd* is not sufficient for one to be a Muslim, as the disbelievers in the time of our Prophet Muḥammad (ﷺ) acknowledged this type of *Tawḥīd*, but still that did not enter them into Islām. The reason is because they still directed acts of worship to other than Allāh. Because of that, Allāh and His messenger deemed them to be disbelievers.

Allāh commanded His Prophet Muḥammad (ﷺ) to say to them:

﴿ قُلۡ مَن يَرۡزُقُكُم مِّنَ ٱلسَّمَآءِ وَٱلۡأَرۡضِ أَمَّن يَمۡلِكُ ٱلسَّمۡعَ وَٱلۡأَبۡصَٰرَ وَمَن يُخۡرِجُ ٱلۡحَيَّ مِنَ ٱلۡمَيِّتِ وَيُخۡرِجُ ٱلۡمَيِّتَ مِنَ ٱلۡحَيِّ وَمَن يُدَبِّرُ ٱلۡأَمۡرَۚ فَسَيَقُولُونَ ٱللَّهُۚ فَقُلۡ أَفَلَا تَتَّقُونَ ٣١ ﴾

"Say, "Who provides for you from the heaven and the earth? Or who controls hearing and sight and who brings the living out of the dead and brings the dead out of the living and who arranges [every] matter?" They will say "Allāh", so say, "Then will you not fear Him?"

[*Yūnus* 10:31]

This verse shows you that the disbelievers already affirmed Allāh's actions (*al-Rubūbiyyah*) and knew that He had no partner in those matters. But even with this, they turned acts of worship, such as seeking blessings, supplication, and prayer to other than Allāh.

They directed them towards saints and righteous men, stones, trees, and other false deities, believing they could bring benefit to them or intercede for them with Allāh. These were some of the false beliefs that Allāh sent His Messengers to eliminate, because all of that constitutes setting up rivals, equals and partners with Allāh.

2. *Tawḥīd al-Ulūhiyyah* or *Tawḥīd* of worship. This is to have belief that Allāh is the only One worshipped *in truth* and that He has no partners in that. One can also say it is that the servants single out Allāh with their actions, such as *du'a'* (supplication), *nadhr* (vowing), *dhabḥ* (slaughtering), *khawf* (fear), *tawwakul* (placing your trust), and every other type of worship that Allāh commanded with.

So all acts of worship must be directed to Allāh alone. This is the type of *Tawḥīd* that the Messengers came with and the reason why Allāh sent down the Books of revelation; so that all worship be directed sincerely and solely to Allāh.

Allāh said:

﴿ ۞ وَٱعۡبُدُواْ ٱللَّهَ وَلَا تُشۡرِكُواْ بِهِۦ شَيۡـٔٗاۖ ﴾

"Worship Allāh, and join none in partners along with Him." [*al-Nisā'* 4:36]

And He said:

﴿ وَمَآ أَرۡسَلۡنَا مِن قَبۡلِكَ مِن رَّسُولٍ إِلَّا نُوحِيٓ إِلَيۡهِ أَنَّهُۥ لَآ إِلَٰهَ إِلَّآ
أَنَا۠ فَٱعۡبُدُونِ ٢٥ ﴾

"And We sent not before you any Messenger except that We revealed to him that: There is no deity (in truth) except Me, so worship Me." [*al-Anbiyā* 21:25]

And:

﴿ وَلَقَدۡ بَعَثۡنَا فِي كُلِّ أُمَّةٖ رَّسُولًا أَنِ ٱعۡبُدُواْ ٱللَّهَ وَٱجۡتَنِبُواْ
ٱلطَّٰغُوتَۖ ﴾

"And We certainly sent to every nation a messenger, [saying]: Worship Allāh and avoid Ṭāghūt (i.e. false deities)." [*al-Naḥl* 16:36]

This type of *Tawḥīd* is where the disputes between the Messengers and their nations occurred, not the *Tawḥīd al-Rubūbiyyah*, as the majority of mankind recognizes that the Creator is one in His actions, but many fail to single Him out with all acts of worship.

Ibn Kathīr (رَحِمَهُ ٱللَّهُ) stated:

> "All the types of worship which Allāh commanded like Islām, *Īmān*, and *iḥsān* (perfection of worship), and from that is invocation (*du'ā'*), reverential fear (*khawf*), hope and longing (*rajā'*), trust and reliance (*tawakkul*), fervent desire (*raghbah*), dread (*rahbah*), reverence and humility (*khushū'*), awe (*khashyah*), turning repentantly (*inābah*), appealing for aid and assistance (*isti'ānah*), seeking refuge (*isti'ādhah*), seeking deliverance and rescue (*istighāthah*), sacrificing (*dhabḥ*), vows (*nadhr*), and the rest of the types of worship commanded by Allāh, all of them are to be done exclusively for Allāh, the Most High...[1]"

3. *Tawḥīd al-Asmā' wa al-Ṣifāt* or *Tawḥīd* of Allāh's Names and Attributes. This is to have belief in all the Names and Attributes of Allāh that have been reported in the *Qur'ān* or authentic *aḥādīth*. So one only affirms those Names and Attributes of Allāh that He has affirmed for Himself in the *Qur'ān*, or what His Messenger affirmed for Him in his authentic *Sunnah*, without distorting them, denying them, asking how and without resembling Allāh to His creation. A

---

[1] Taken from the translation of the Three Fundamental Principles with the translation of Abu Talha Dawud Burbank (رَحِمَهُ ٱللَّهُ).

person does not give Allāh a name, description, or attribute that He has not named or described Himself with, nor does one deny or reject what He has named Himself or described Himself with, whilst at the same time maintaining the belief that there is nothing similar to Him, the Most High, Free of imperfections.

[Proofs]:

Allāh says in the *Qur'ān*,

﴿لَيْسَ كَمِثْلِهِۦ شَىْءٌ ۖ وَهُوَ ٱلسَّمِيعُ ٱلْبَصِيرُ﴾

"There is nothing like unto Him, and He is the all Hearing, the all Seer." [*al-Shūrā* 42:11]

He also says:

﴿وَلِلَّهِ ٱلْأَسْمَآءُ ٱلْحُسْنَىٰ فَٱدْعُوهُ بِهَا ۖ وَذَرُوا۟ ٱلَّذِينَ يُلْحِدُونَ فِىٓ أَسْمَٰٓئِهِۦ ۚ سَيُجْزَوْنَ مَا كَانُوا۟ يَعْمَلُونَ ﴿١٨٠﴾﴾

"And to Allāh belongs the best names, so invoke Him by them. And leave [the company] of those who practice deviation concerning His names. They will be recompensed for what they have been doing." [*al-A'rāf* 7:180]

He also says:

﴿قُلْ هُوَ ٱللَّهُ أَحَدٌ ۝١ ٱللَّهُ ٱلصَّمَدُ ۝٢ لَمْ يَلِدْ وَلَمْ
يُولَدْ ۝٣ وَلَمْ يَكُن لَّهُۥ كُفُوًا أَحَدٌۢ ۝٤﴾

> **"Say: He is Allāh [who is] One. The Self-Sufficient Master, Whom all creatures need. He has no offspring nor was He born. And there is none co-equal or comparable unto Him."** [*al-Ikhlāṣ* 112:1-4]

Some examples of the Names of Allāh:

Al-Raḥmān- the Most Merciful
Al-Raḥīm- the Bestower of Mercy
Al-Samīʿ- the All Hearer
Al-Baṣīr- the All Seer

Al-"Alīm- the All Knowing
Al-Ghafūr- the Oft-Forgiving

Some examples of Allāh's attributes:

Al-Ḥayāt- He has perfect life (not preceded by death or non-existence and will never die).

Al-ʿUluww- Highness above His creation.
Al-Wajh- He has a Face (not like the face of the creation).
Al-Yad- He has a Hand (not like the hand of His creation).
Al-Nuzūl- He descends (in a manner befitting His Majesty).
Al-Kalām- He speaks (how He wishes and whenever He wishes).
Al-Istiwāʾ- He rose above His throne (in a manner befitting His Majesty).

Chapter Five
Shirk and Some of its Manifestations (Associating Partners with Allāh)

Dear Muslim, there is nothing more harmful and nothing greater in sin than *Shirk*, and it is the greatest thing from which Allāh prohibited mankind. *Shirk* is to set up a partner or equal with Allāh in His worship. This is the sin that Allāh will never forgive, if a person dies upon it. It is the opposite of *Tawḥīd*.

[Proofs]:

Allāh says:

﴿ إِنَّ ٱللَّهَ لَا يَغْفِرُ أَن يُشْرَكَ بِهِۦ وَيَغْفِرُ مَا دُونَ ذَٰلِكَ لِمَن يَشَآءُ ۚ
وَمَن يُشْرِكْ بِٱللَّهِ فَقَدْ ضَلَّ ضَلَٰلًۢا بَعِيدًا ﴿١١٦﴾ ﴾

"Verily, Allāh does not forgive that partners be set up with Him in worship, but He forgives what is less than that to whomsoever He wills."
[*Al-Nisā'* 4:116]

He also says:

﴿ لَقَدْ كَفَرَ ٱلَّذِينَ قَالُوٓا۟ إِنَّ ٱللَّهَ هُوَ ٱلْمَسِيحُ ٱبْنُ مَرْيَمَ ۖ وَقَالَ
ٱلْمَسِيحُ يَٰبَنِىٓ إِسْرَٰٓءِيلَ ٱعْبُدُوا۟ ٱللَّهَ رَبِّى وَرَبَّكُمْ ۖ إِنَّهُۥ مَن يُشْرِكْ بِٱللَّهِ

فَقَدْ حَرَّمَ ٱللَّهُ عَلَيْهِ ٱلْجَنَّةَ وَمَأْوَىٰهُ ٱلنَّارُ ۖ وَمَا لِلظَّٰلِمِينَ مِنْ

أَنصَارٍ ﴿٧٢﴾

"Those have disbelieved who say that Allāh is the messiah, son of Maryam. The messiah said nothing but "O children of Israel, worship Allāh, my Lord and your Lord." Verily he who associates partners with Allāh, then Allāh has made Paradise prohibited for him, and his abode will be the Hellfire and the wrongdoers will have no helpers." [*Al-Ma'idah* 5:72]

He also says:

﴿ وَلَقَدْ أُوحِىَ إِلَيْكَ وَإِلَى ٱلَّذِينَ مِن قَبْلِكَ لَئِنْ أَشْرَكْتَ لَيَحْبَطَنَّ

عَمَلُكَ وَلَتَكُونَنَّ مِنَ ٱلْخَٰسِرِينَ ﴿٦٥﴾

"If you were to commit Shirk (with Allāh), He will make all of your good deeds null and void and you will be from the losers." [*Al-Zumar* 39:65]

So with this it becomes clear that "*Shirk*[1] destroys one's Islām, nullifies deeds, and the one who commits it, then no good deed will ever be accepted from him, and he will not be forgiven for any deed.

[1] This is referring to major *Shirk*.

He can never be hopeful of being saved from the hell-fire, rather he will abide therein forever."[1]

Shirk is of two categories, Major and Minor.

An example of Major *Shirk* is to wear a ring, bracelet or string to repel or ward off calamites, or wearing amulets or charms to bring about benefit, believing that these things independently repel harm or bestow good, and not Allāh. In the *Qur'ān*, Allāh refutes those who carry such false beliefs. He says:

﴿ وَلَئِن سَأَلْتَهُم مَّنْ خَلَقَ السَّمَاوَاتِ وَالْأَرْضَ لَيَقُولُنَّ اللَّهُ ۚ قُلْ
أَفَرَأَيْتُم مَّا تَدْعُونَ مِن دُونِ اللَّهِ إِنْ أَرَادَنِيَ اللَّهُ بِضُرٍّ هَلْ هُنَّ
كَاشِفَاتُ ضُرِّهِ أَوْ أَرَادَنِي بِرَحْمَةٍ هَلْ هُنَّ مُمْسِكَاتُ رَحْمَتِهِ ۚ
قُلْ حَسْبِيَ اللَّهُ ۖ عَلَيْهِ يَتَوَكَّلُ الْمُتَوَكِّلُونَ ﴿٣٨﴾ ﴾

> **"Say: Tell me then, the things that you invoke besides Allāh, if Allāh intended some harm for me, could they remove His harm, or if He intended some mercy for me could they withhold His Mercy? Say: "Sufficient for me is Allāh; in Him those who trust put their trust."**
> [*Al-Zumar* 39:38]

Also from major *Shirk* is to make a vow, slaughter, or sacrifice for other than Allāh.

---

[11] From explanation of *al-Wajibāt* (p. 101) by Shaykh Aḥmad al-Najmī, may Allah have mercy on him.

Also from major *shirk* is to invoke or supplicate to other than Allāh, such as supplicating to a person in a grave, supplicating to a person who was known to be righteous, or to a prophet or an angel. Allāh rebukes those who supplicate to those besides Him. He said in the *Qur'ān*:

﴿ يُولِجُ ٱلَّيۡلَ فِي ٱلنَّهَارِ وَيُولِجُ ٱلنَّهَارَ فِي ٱلَّيۡلِ وَسَخَّرَ ٱلشَّمۡسَ
وَٱلۡقَمَرَ كُلّٞ يَجۡرِي لِأَجَلٖ مُّسَمّٗىۚ ذَٰلِكُمُ ٱللَّهُ رَبُّكُمۡ لَهُ ٱلۡمُلۡكُۚ
وَٱلَّذِينَ تَدۡعُونَ مِن دُونِهِۦ مَا يَمۡلِكُونَ مِن قِطۡمِيرٍ ١٣ إِن
تَدۡعُوهُمۡ لَا يَسۡمَعُواْ دُعَآءَكُمۡ وَلَوۡ سَمِعُواْ مَا ٱسۡتَجَابُواْ لَكُمۡۖ وَيَوۡمَ ٱلۡقِيَٰمَةِ
يَكۡفُرُونَ بِشِرۡكِكُمۡۚ وَلَا يُنَبِّئُكَ مِثۡلُ خَبِيرٖ ١٤ ﴾

> **"And those whom you invoke or call upon instead of Him, own not even a Qitmīr (i.e. the thin membrane that covers the seed of a date). If you invoke (or call upon) them they do not hear your call, and if they could hear it, they could not grant (your request), and on the day of resurrection they will disown your worshipping of them. And none can inform you like Him who is the All-Knower (of each and everything)."** [*Al-Fāṭir* 35:13-14]

Also from major *shirk* is to seek aid, rescue, or deliverance from other than Allāh in matters that only Allāh can aid you in or grant you rescue. All of these things expel a person from Islām, nullify their good deeds, and land them in the Hellfire forever, if they die without repenting.

An example of minor *shirk* is that one seeks by his acts of worship to be praised by the people. This is known as *Riyā'*. The Prophet (صَلَّى ٱللَّهُ عَلَيْهِ وَعَلَىٰ آلِهِ وَسَلَّمَ) also termed this inconspicuous (hidden) *shirk*.

Prophet Muḥammad (صَلَّى ٱللَّهُ عَلَيْهِ وَعَلَىٰ آلِهِ وَسَلَّمَ) said:

> "Shall I not inform you of what I fear most for you more than the Anti-Christ? They said certainly. He said it is the hidden *shirk*; a person stands and prays and beautifies his prayer because he sees a person looking at him."[1]

Also from minor *shirk* is that a person swears by other than Allāh, such as the statement of some people, I swear by the Prophet, or I swear by my father, or children.

Prophet Muḥammad (صَلَّى ٱللَّهُ عَلَيْهِ وَعَلَىٰ آلِهِ وَسَلَّمَ) said:

> "Do not swear by your fathers. Whoever swears by Allāh let him be truthful…"[2]

He also said:

> "Whoever swears by other than Allāh has committed *shirk* or *kufr*."

Also from minor *shirk* is that a person says, "If it wasn't for so and so, such and such wouldn't have happened", or "If it wasn't for such and such, then such and such matter wouldn't have happened."

---

[1] Reported by Aḥmad in his *Musnad* and declared *ḥasan* by Shaykh al-Albānī. See *Ṣaḥīḥ al-Jāmi'* (no. 2604).

[2] Reported by Ibn Mājah and declared *Ṣaḥīḥ* by Shaykh al-Albānī in *Ṣaḥīḥ al Jāmi'* (no. 7124).

What is upon the Muslim to say is "If it wasn't for Allāh alone…", and it is permissible to say "If it wasn't for Allāh, then so and so."

So O Muslim! This matter of *shirk* is very serious and dangerous; it is upon you to know what *shirk* is, major and minor, in order to stay away from it. Allāh does not forgive the one who dies upon major *shirk*. Also, the action which is mixed with minor *shirk*, such as *riyā*, is rejected and not accepted by Allāh.

Chapter Six
Pillars of Islām in Brief

The pillars of Islām are five.

[Proof]:

Prophet Muḥammad (صَلَّى ٱللَّهُ عَلَيْهِ وَعَلَىٰ آلِهِ وَسَلَّمَ) said:

> "Islām is built upon five: the testimony that none has the right to be worshipped except Allāh and Muḥammad is the Messenger of Allāh, to establish the prayer, to pay the *Zakāt*, to fast in *Ramaḍān*, and to make the *Ḥajj* to the house of Allāh."

Reported by al-Bukhārī and Muslim.

The First Pillar- the testimony of *Lā ilāha illa Allāh* (none has the right to be worshipped in truth except Allāh) *Wa Anna Muhammad Rasūl Allāh* [and Muhammad is the Messenger of Allāh].

These two testimonies are the foundation of all foundations, and the rest of the pillars follow them. So the rest of the pillars or any other deeds are of no benefit if they are not based upon these two testimonies. These testimonies go hand in hand and do not separate, so it is a must to testify that Muḥammad is the Messenger of Allāh, along with the testimony that none has the right to be worshipped except Allāh.

The testimony "none has the right to be worshipped except Allāh" necessitates that only Allāh be worshipped, and the testimony

"Muḥammad is the Messenger of Allāh" necessitates that worship be done in accordance to what the Messenger of Allāh came with.[1]

The Second Pillar- to establish the prayer.

The prayer is the second most important pillar of Islām and it is the strong bond between the servant and his Lord. It will be the first thing that a person will be asked about on the Day of Resurrection, and it distinguishes the Muslim from the disbeliever.

There are five obligatory prayers in Islām that occur throughout the day and the night. They are:

(1) *Ẓuhr* (i.e. the noon prayer)
(2) *'Asr* (i.e. the afternoon prayer)
(3) *Maghrib* (i.e. the prayer after sunset)
(4) *'Ishā'* (i.e. the prayer when night falls)
(5) *Fajr* (i.e. the prayer when dawn first enters)

The Third Pillar- to pay the *Zakāt*.

Zakāt is an act of worship done connected to wealth, and its benefit is not restricted for the one who pays it, rather it is a benefit to other Muslims. Allāh made the *Zakāt* obligatory upon the wealth of the rich to be paid to the poor Muslims in a manner that will benefit the poor, but not harm the rich.

---

[1] Explanation of 40 *ḥadīth* (p. 106) by *Shaykh* 'Abd al-Muḥsin al-'Abbād al-Badr.

This is because it is a minor portion of a person's wealth.[1] *Zakāt* purifies the Muslim from stinginess and is comfort for the poor and needy Muslims.

The Fourth Pillar- Fasting the month of *Ramaḍān*.

Ramaḍān is the 9th month on the Islāmic calendar. Allāh has made fasting this month obligatory upon every Muslim who has reached the age of puberty, is of sound intellect, healthy, and residing in their hometown (i.e. not travelling).

Fasting is an act of worship which is done for Allāh alone by withholding from food, drink, sexual intercourse and anything that breaks the fast, from the time of *Fajr* (dawn prayer) until the time of *Maghrib* (sunset). Fasting is a purification of the soul by having abstinence from the worldly desires, and it causes one to have sympathy for the poor and to feel some of what they feel from hunger pains and thirst.

Fasting is beloved to Allāh because of the secrecy contained in it. No one knows who is truly fasting except Allāh, and for this reason Allāh rewards the fasting person without limit.

The Fifth Pillar- Performing the *Ḥajj*.

The *Ḥajj* is an act of worship that requires bodily actions and wealth alike. Allāh has made the *Ḥajj* obligatory once in one's lifetime for the one who has the means, is physically able to perform it, and finds transportation to Makkah.

---

[1] Explanation of 40 *ḥadīth* (p. 107) by *Shaykh* ʿAbd al-Muḥsin al-ʿAbbād al-Badr.

From the intents of *Ḥajj* is that Allāh is worshipped in those places where He commanded that He be worshipped (i.e. in Makkah, *'Arafah*, *Muzdalifah*, and *Minā*). From its benefits is that Muslims gather from all places around the globe in one place, all considered equal with no distinction between the rich and poor, black and white, rulers or ruled, in order to worship Allāh alone and perform the rituals that He commanded with. The one who performs the *Ḥajj* with sincerity and according to the *Sunnah* of Prophet Muḥammad (صَلَّى اللَّهُ عَلَيْهِ وَعَلَى آلِهِ وَسَلَّمَ) will return home like the day when his mother gave birth to him (i.e. free of sin).

Chapter Seven
Pillars of Īmān in Brief

The pillars of *Īmān* are six. The proof for this is the *ḥadīth* of Jibrīl. In this *ḥadīth* the angel Jibrīl (Gabriel) came in the form of a man and asked Prophet Muḥammad about matters of the religion in order to teach the people. In the *ḥadīth* he asked the Prophet, "Inform me about *Īmān*." The Prophet (صَلَّى ٱللَّهُ عَلَيْهِ وَعَلَىٰ آلِهِ وَسَلَّمَ) answered by saying: "It is that you believe in Allāh, His Angels, His Books, His Messengers, the Last Day, and that you believe in the divine decree, the good of it and the bad of it." Reported in *Ṣaḥīḥ* Muslim.

The First- Belief in Allāh: Belief in Allāh is the foundation of everything that one must have belief in. Whoever does not believe in Allāh does not believe in the rest of the pillars of *Īmān*, and for this reason belief in the Angels, Books, and Messengers were all attributed to Allāh [i.e. it is said **His** Angels, **His** Books and **His** Messengers].

To believe in Allāh firstly means to believe in His existence and that He is the One who brought everything into existence. He is the First and there is nothing before Him, and He is the Last, there is nothing after Him. Also belief in Allāh means that you believe in His *Rubūbiyyah* (Lordship), His *Ulūhiyyah* (that He is deserving all worship), and that you belief in His Beautiful Names and Lofty Attributes.

The Second- Belief in His Angels: This is to believe that the Angels are a creation that Allāh created from light. They have wings, some with two, three, and four. It has been reported that Angel Jibrīl has six hundred wings.

The Angels are of a great number and no one knows their number except Allāh. They do not have a will to disobey Allāh and they do everything that Allāh commands them. The Angels have been delegated with duties such as delivering revelation, bringing down the rain drops, taking people's souls at the time of death and many other duties. It is obligatory to believe and deem truthful all the information that has come in the *Qur'ān* and *Sunnah* regarding the Angels.

The Third-Belief in His Books: Belief in the Books is to believe and deem truthful every Book that Allāh sent down upon His Messengers and believe that they are truth, and they are the uncreated speech of Allāh. They entail what is needed for the happiness of mankind; and whoever adheres to them will be successful, and whoever turns away from them will be at a great loss.

From those Books are the *Injīl*, *Tawrāt*, *Zabūr*, and the final revelation that was sent to Muḥammad, the *Qur'ān*. The *Qur'ān* is the everlasting miracle that Allāh sent Muḥammad with in which He took upon Himself to preserve and guard from plagiarism and distortion. The *Qur'ān* is an authority over and an abrogation of the previous Books sent by Allāh.

The Fourth- Belief in His Messengers: Belief in the Messengers means to have firm belief and attestation that Allāh has raised individuals from mankind as Prophets and Messengers who direct people to the truth, and call them from the darkness of misguidance, *shirk*, and disobedience to the light of guidance, *Tawḥīd*, and obedience to Allāh.

The Messengers were tasked to convey the legislations that were sent down to them, and they all conveyed what they were tasked to convey in the best and most complete manner. There are twenty five Messengers mentioned in the *Qur'ān*, eighteen of them were mentioned in *Sūrah al-An'ām* 6:83-86.

Some of the names of the Messengers sent by Allāh are Ādam, Nūḥ (Noah), Ibrāhīm (Abraham), Mūsā (Moses), 'Īsā (Jesus), and Muḥammad, may Allāh's peace and salutations be upon them all. There were also Messengers whom Allāh sent whom He did not mention to us. We still must believe in them in a general sense.

The Fifth-Belief in the Last day: Belief in the Last Day entails firm belief and attestation of everything that has come in the *Qur'ān* and *Sunnah* of that which will occur after death. This includes the punishment or bliss that will occur in the grave, resurrection from the grave when Allāh commands the Angel to blow in the trumpet at the end of time, and that all the people will be gathered to one place to stand in front of Allāh to be questioned.

It also entails matters such as the reckoning for one's deeds, the deeds being weighed, crossing over the bridge that will be placed over the Hellfire and having belief in the Paradise prepared for those who believed in Allāh and did righteous deeds and the Hellfire prepared for those who disbelieved in Allāh and did wicked deeds, and those who disobeyed Him. Both Paradise and Hellfire are created and exist now.

The Sixth- Belief in the divine decree (al-Qadr): Belief in the divine decree is to believe that Allāh decreed everything that will occur until the Day of Resurrection. This belief includes four matters:

(1) That Allāh has infinite knowledge of everything that will occur.
(2) That Allāh has written everything that has been decreed.
(3) That Allāh has willed to occur everything that takes place.

(4) That Allāh created everything in existence in accordance to His infinite knowledge, His writing, and His will.[1]

Prophet Muḥammad (صَلَّىٰ ٱللَّهُ عَلَيْهِ وَعَلَىٰ آلِهِ وَسَلَّمَ) said:

> "Whatever passed you was never going to befall you, and whatever befalls you was never going to pass you."

So it is obligatory to believe in these four levels of the divine decree and that everything that Allāh wills must come into existence and whatever He did not will can never come into existence.

---

[1] Explanation of 40 *ḥadīth* (p. 102) by *Shaykh* 'Abd al-Muḥsin al-'Abbād al-Badr (p. 102).

Chapter Eight
Īmān [Faith] Consists of Statement, Action And Belief

Dear Muslim, *Īmān* [faith] has a tremendous status in the religion and has countless benefits that the believer reaps in this life and the next. For this reason, Allāh commanded with having *Īmān* in many places in His Book and has coupled that with performing righteous actions. In the *Qur'ān*, He addresses the believers with the beautiful address: "O you who believe" ninety times. He has informed that those who possess *Īmān,* that He will grant them a good life and grant them the reward of Paradise. Allāh says:

﴿ مَنْ عَمِلَ صَٰلِحًا مِّن ذَكَرٍ أَوْ أُنثَىٰ وَهُوَ مُؤْمِنٌ فَلَنُحْيِيَنَّهُۥ حَيَوٰةً طَيِّبَةً ۖ وَلَنَجْزِيَنَّهُمْ أَجْرَهُم بِأَحْسَنِ مَا كَانُوا۟ يَعْمَلُونَ ﴿٩٧﴾ ﴾

"Whoever works righteousness, whether male or female, while he (or she) is a true believer (i.e. having Īmān) verily, to him We will give a good life, and We shall pay them certainly a reward in proportion to the best of what they used to do (i.e. Paradise in the hereafter)." [*Al-Naḥl* 16:97]

And He said:

﴿ إِنَّ ٱلَّذِينَ ءَامَنُوا۟ وَعَمِلُوا۟ ٱلصَّٰلِحَٰتِ كَانَتْ لَهُمْ جَنَّٰتُ ٱلْفِرْدَوْسِ نُزُلًا ﴿١٠٧﴾ ﴾

"Verily! Those who believe (i.e. having Īmān) and do righteous deeds, shall have the Gardens

of the Paradise for their entertainment." [*al-Kahf* 18:107]

So a person is not given anything better from Allāh than having *Īmān*, not wealth, status, children, or anything else.

The proper belief of the Muslims in regards to *Īmān* is that it consists of statement upon the tongue, belief of the heart, and actions upon the limbs; it increases with obedience to Allāh, and it decreases with disobedience to Allāh. These are important fundamentals that the Muslim must understand.

Shaykh al-Islām Ibn Taymiyyah said in his book *al-'Aqīdah al-Wāsiṭiyyah*:

> "And from the fundamentals of the *Ahl al-Sunnah wa al-Jamā'ah* is that the religion and *Īmān* is statement and action; statement of the heart and tongue, and action of the heart, tongue, and limbs."

Shaykh Ṣāliḥ al-Fawzān says explaining the words of Ibn Taymiyyah:

> "So statement of the heart is the (sound) belief held within the heart and the statement of the tongue is to speak the word of Islām (i.e. the *Shahādah*). Likewise, action is of two types: action of the heart, which is intention and sincerity, and action of the limbs- meaning what is done with the body parts, such as prayer, *Ḥajj*, and *Jihād*.
>
> The difference between the statements of the heart and its actions, is that its statements is the matters of belief in which one acknowledges and believes. As for the actions of the heart,

> what is intended is its motions which Allāh and His messenger loves, such as having a love for good, its strong will-power, having a hatred for evil and being determined to abandon it.
>
> Thus, the actions of the heart results in actions of the limbs and statements upon the tongue. Therefore, statements of the tongue and actions of the limbs are part of *Īmān*."[1]

So the above shows us that *Īmān* consists of statements, such as the utterance of the two testimonies of faith upon the tongue, actions, such as the prayer, fasting, *Ḥajj*, and other obligatory and recommended actions. It also consists of belief of the heart, meaning that one holds firm and true belief in all matters that Allāh commanded the Muslims to believe in, at the head of them the six pillars of *Īmān*.

Some groups that ascribe to Islām have went astray as it relates to the correct definition and reality of *Īmān*, and they can be categorized into four groups:

The First: Those who say that *Īmān* is only awareness of Allāh, even if there is no attestation of the heart (*taṣdīq*). This is the most heinous and evil statement regarding the definition of *Īmān,* and it is pure disbelief.

This is because the heads of disbelief such as Iblīs (i.e. the devil), Firʿawn and his chief Hāmān and Qārūn all had awareness of Allāh in their hearts. However, because they did not pronounce (*Īmān*) upon their tongues, nor did they attest to it within their hearts and did not act upon it with their limbs, this awareness was of no benefit to them.

---

[1] *Sharḥ al-ʿAqīdah al-Wāsiṭiyyah* (p. 179).

Allāh says:

﴿ وَجَحَدُوا۟ بِهَا وَٱسْتَيْقَنَتْهَآ أَنفُسُهُمْ ظُلْمًا وَعُلُوًّا ﴾

> **"And they belied them (those āyāt) wrongfully and arrogantly, though their ownselves were convinced thereof."** [*Al-Naml* 27:14]

The Second: Those who say that *Īmān* is belief in the heart without statement of the tongue and actions of the limbs. This is also incorrect, as it would mean that the disbelievers such as the Jews and Christians are upon *Īmān*, as they attest with their heart to matters of belief. Allāh says in the *Qur'ān*:

﴿ ٱلَّذِينَ ءَاتَيْنَـٰهُمُ ٱلْكِتَـٰبَ يَعْرِفُونَهُۥ كَمَا يَعْرِفُونَ أَبْنَآءَهُمْ ۖ وَإِنَّ فَرِيقًا
مِّنْهُمْ لَيَكْتُمُونَ ٱلْحَقَّ وَهُمْ يَعْلَمُونَ ١٤٦ ﴾

> **"Those to whom We gave the Scripture (Jews and Christians) recognize him (i.e. Muḥammad) as they recognize their sons. But verily a party of them conceal the truth while they know it."** [*al-Baqarah* 2:146]

Something noteworthy of mentioning while discussing this second type, is that some misinformed Muslims use the argument that belief is merely in the heart when they are given advice upon some of their shortcomings or their lack of implementation of what Allāh made obligatory upon them.

You find some of them respond when they are advised of some of these matters, "Allāh knows what is in my heart", or "Only Allāh can judge what is in my heart". These statements contain truth, but what is intended by them is to leave off censuring and rebuking open acts of disobedience, innovation, and other matters they commit which contradict the lofty Religion of Islām.[1]

You previously read the statement of *Shaykh* Ṣāliḥ al-Fawzān, "Thus the actions of the heart results in actions of the limbs and statements upon the tongue."

Further, the Prophet (صَلَّى ٱللَّهُ عَلَيْهِ وَسَلَّمَ) clearly alluded to this in statement: "Indeed in the body is a morsel of flesh, if it is upright then the rest of the body will be upright, and if it is corrupt, the rest of the body will be corrupt, and it is the heart."

So this shows us that whatever is present in the heart it is a must that it be manifested upon the tongue and limbs.

---

[1] *Shaykh* Muḥammad Nāṣir al-Dīn al-Albānī (رَحِمَهُ ٱللَّهُ) mentions in the introduction of his checking of *Riyāḍ al-Ṣāliḥīn*, *ḥadīth* number 8 in the book which is the *ḥadīth* of Abu Hurayrah (رَضِيَ ٱللَّهُ عَنْهُ) that states that the Prophet (صَلَّى ٱللَّهُ عَلَيْهِ وَسَلَّمَ) said: "Indeed Allah does not look at your bodies nor your physical images, but he looks at your hearts" Collected by Muslim. *Shaykh* al-Albānī says, "Imām Muslim and others collect an additional wording (which is) 'and your actions'..." *Shaykh* Albānī continues, "And this addition is very important, because many people understand this *ḥadīth* incorrectly. When you command them with what the legislation has commanded them with, such as growing the beard, leaving off imitating the disbelievers and other than that from the affairs commanded by the legislation, they reply to you by saying what is considered is only what is in the heart. They support their claim with this *ḥadīth* without knowing of the authentic addition (i.e. "and your actions") that shows that Allāh, the Majestic and High, also looks at the actions; if they are righteous He accepts them and if not He rejects them, as many evidences prove.." *Riyāḍ al-Ṣāliḥīn* with *Shaykh* al-Albānī's checking (p. 21-22).

The Third: Those who say that *Īmān* is only statement upon the tongue, even if one does not attest to it in the heart. This is also a statement of falsehood as it would mean that the hypocrites possess *Īmān*, whereas Allāh informed that the hypocrites are in the lowest depths of the hell-fire.

They also pronounce the two testimonies of faith upon the tongue and perform acts of worship with their limbs, but they do not believe that sincerely within their hearts.

Allāh says:

﴿إِذَا جَآءَكَ ٱلْمُنَٰفِقُونَ قَالُوا۟ نَشْهَدُ إِنَّكَ لَرَسُولُ ٱللَّهِ ۗ وَٱللَّهُ يَعْلَمُ إِنَّكَ لَرَسُولُهُۥ وَٱللَّهُ يَشْهَدُ إِنَّ ٱلْمُنَٰفِقِينَ لَكَٰذِبُونَ ﴿١﴾﴾

> **"When the hypocrites come to you they say: 'We bear witness that you are indeed the Messenger of Allāh.' Allāh knows that you are indeed His Messenger and Allāh bears witness that the hypocrites are liars."** [*al-Munāfiqūn* 63:1]

He also said regarding them:

﴿يَقُولُونَ بِأَلْسِنَتِهِم مَّا لَيْسَ فِى قُلُوبِهِمْ ۚ﴾

> **"They say with their tongues what is not in their hearts."** [*Al-Fatḥ* 48:11]

The fourth: Those who say that *Īmān* is belief in the heart and statement upon the tongue, but they do not consider actions as part of *Īmān*, and this is also incorrect.[1]

The Prophet (صَلَّى ٱللَّهُ عَلَيْهِ وَسَلَّمَ) said:

> "*Īmān* is seventy some odd branches. The highest is the statement *Lā ilāha illa Allāh*, and the lowest is to remove something harmful from the pathway. Shyness is also a branch of *Īmān*."

Collected by Bukhārī and Muslim.

So here the Prophet (صَلَّى ٱللَّهُ عَلَيْهِ وَسَلَّمَ) included removing something harmful from the pathway to be a part of *Īmān*, and that is an action. There are many other evidences that prove that actions are a part of *Īmān*.

As for the fact that *Īmān* increases and decreases, there are a number of evidences to support this in the *Qur'ān* and *Sunnah*. We will mention a few:

Allāh said:

﴿ٱلَّذِينَ قَالَ لَهُمُ ٱلنَّاسُ إِنَّ ٱلنَّاسَ قَدْ جَمَعُوا۟ لَكُمْ فَٱخْشَوْهُمْ
فَزَادَهُمْ إِيمَٰنًا وَقَالُوا۟ حَسْبُنَا ٱللَّهُ وَنِعْمَ ٱلْوَكِيلُ ١٧٣﴾

> **"Those unto whom the people (i.e. hypocrites) said: Verily the people (disbelievers) have gathered against you (a great army), therefore**

[1] Taken from the book *Masā'il fī al-Īmān* by *Shaykh* Ṣāliḥ al-Fawzān (p. 18-19).

fear them. But it only increased them in faith and they said: Allāh (alone) is sufficient for us, and He is the Best Disposer of affairs (for us).” [Āl-ʿImrān 3:173]

And He said:

﴿ إِنَّمَا ٱلْمُؤْمِنُونَ ٱلَّذِينَ إِذَا ذُكِرَ ٱللَّهُ وَجِلَتْ قُلُوبُهُمْ وَإِذَا تُلِيَتْ
عَلَيْهِمْ ءَايَٰتُهُۥ زَادَتْهُمْ إِيمَٰنًا وَعَلَىٰ رَبِّهِمْ يَتَوَكَّلُونَ ﴿٢﴾ ﴾

“The believers are only those who when Allāh is mentioned, feel a fear in their hearts and when His verses are recited unto them, they increase them in faith, and they put their trust in their Lord.” [*Al-Anfāl* 8:2]

Lastly we would like to mention some things that causes the *Īmān* to increase and things that causes the *Īmān* to decrease.

Some causes for the increase of *Īmān*:

1. Learning beneficial knowledge of the religion.
2. Reciting the *Qur'ān* and pondering over its verses.
3. Knowing and understanding the Beautiful Names and Lofty Attributes of Allāh.
4. Being diligent in performing acts of worship and obedience.

Some causes for the decrease of *Īmān*:

1. Ignorance of the religion.
2. Committing sins and acts of disobedience.

3. Chasing the temptations of the worldly life and materialistic things.
4. Bad companionship.

Chapter Nine
Conditions of Lā ilāha illa Allāh

The statement of the *Shahādah* (*La ilāha illa Allāh*) has seven conditions:

1. Knowledge. One must have knowledge of what this statement affirms and what it negates. It affirms worship for Allāh alone and negates the right of worship for everyone and everything besides Allāh. If one does not have knowledge of this statement then it is easy for them to fall into what negates and invalidates it, such as the worship of other than Allāh.

2. Certainty. This is that the one who says this statement does so with certainty, not having the least amount of doubt.

3. Sincerity: This is that one has sincerity when pronouncing this statement, only seeking the Face of Allāh. One does not say it to show off or for any worldly gains.

4. Truthfulness. This is to say this statement out of truthfulness which negates lying. People were found to say this statement while they were untruthful, such as the hypocrites.

5. Love. One must have love for the statement *Lā ilāha illa Allāh* and have love for what it points to, and to be happy that Allāh bestowed His favor upon you to say it and believe in it. Likewise, this entails to have love for those who say this statement and support it, aid it and act by it, no matter the color of their skin, their land, or their language.

6. Submission. One must submit to the rights of this statement, and this is by doing the obligatory acts of worship that Allāh commanded us to do.

7. Acceptance. One accepts this statement fully and does not reject it, hoping for the reward of Allāh and seeking His good pleasure.

Chapter Ten
Pillars of Lā ilāha illa Allāh

Lā ilāha illa Allāh has two pillars; affirmation and negation. When you say *Lā ilāha* (i.e. there is no Deity) you are negating the right of worship from everything besides Allāh. When you say *illa Allāh* (i.e. except Allāh), you are affirming the right of worship for Allāh alone. For this reason, the scholars say that the meaning of *Lā ilāha illa Allāh* is, that there is no deity worshipped in truth except Allāh, and if other than Allāh is worshipped, it is done only in falsehood.

Chapter Eleven
The Meaning of Muḥammad Rasūlullāh [Muḥammad is the Messenger of Allāh]

The meaning of Muḥammad is the Messenger of Allāh is to obey him in what he commanded, to deem him truthful regarding everything that he came with and informed of from Allāh, whether that entails what came in the past or what will come in the future, and that one does not worship Allāh except by what he legislated. It also means that he is honored and respected and that we love him more than anyone from the creation.

The Messenger of Allāh (صَلَّى ٱللَّٰهُ عَلَيْهِ وَعَلَىٰ آلِهِ وَسَلَّمَ) stated: "None of you truly believe until I am more beloved to him than his family, his wealth, and all of mankind." Reported by Bukhārī and Muslim.

Further, it is incumbent upon us to believe that Muḥammad (صَلَّى ٱللَّٰهُ عَلَيْهِ وَعَلَىٰ آلِهِ وَسَلَّمَ) was a servant of Allāh and His Messenger and he does not deserve any of the rights that are exclusive to Allāh, such as worship. He neither has absolute knowledge of the unseen. Thus, it is not permissible that the Muslim goes overboard in regards to the Prophet (صَلَّى ٱللَّٰهُ عَلَيْهِ وَعَلَىٰ آلِهِ وَسَلَّمَ).

The Prophet (صَلَّى ٱللَّٰهُ عَلَيْهِ وَعَلَىٰ آلِهِ وَسَلَّمَ) said:

> "Do not go beyond bounds with regards to me as the Christians did with Jesus son of Mary. I am only a slave of Allāh and His messenger."

Reported by Bukhārī and Muslim.

Chapter Twelve
The Nullifiers of Islām

The nullifiers of Islām are those matters that invalidate and corrupt ones Islām. It is possible for the one who embraces Islām and testifies that none deserves the right to be worshipped in truth except Allāh and that Muḥammad is the Messenger of Allāh, to nullify his or her Islām and *Tawḥīd* by committing one of these nullifiers. This may occur whilst a person does not even realize, and thus they apostate from the religion and are counted amongst the disbelievers.[1]

First: Committing *shirk* (associating partners) in the worship of Allāh, the Most High.

Allāh says:

﴿ إِنَّ ٱللَّهَ لَا يَغْفِرُ أَن يُشْرَكَ بِهِۦ وَيَغْفِرُ مَا دُونَ ذَٰلِكَ لِمَن يَشَآءُ ﴾

> **"Verily, Allāh does not forgive that partners be associated with Him in worship, but He forgives what is less than that to whomsoever He wills."** [*Al-Nisā'* 4:116]

And He says:

---

[1] *Shaykh* Ṣāliḥ al-Fawzān in his explanation of the nullifiers of Islām.

﴿ لَقَدْ كَفَرَ ٱلَّذِينَ قَالُوٓا۟ إِنَّ ٱللَّهَ هُوَ ٱلْمَسِيحُ ٱبْنُ مَرْيَمَ ۖ

وَقَالَ ٱلْمَسِيحُ يَٰبَنِىٓ إِسْرَٰٓءِيلَ ٱعْبُدُوا۟ ٱللَّهَ رَبِّى وَرَبَّكُمْ ۖ إِنَّهُۥ ﴾

"Verily, the one who associates partners in worship with Allāh, then He has made Paradise forbidden for him, and his final abode will be the Hellfire, and the wrongdoers will not have any helpers." [*Al-Ma'idah* 5:72]

Also from this is to slaughter for other than Allāh the Most High, such as those who offer sacrifices by slaughtering for the *jinn* or (one in) a grave.

Second: Whoever places intermediaries between himself and Allāh, supplicating to them, asking them for intercession, and placing reliance upon them. This is disbelief according to the agreement of the scholars.

Third: Whoever does not hold the polytheists to be disbelievers, or has doubts about their disbelief or considers their ways and beliefs to be correct, has committed disbelief.

Fourth: Whoever believes that some guidance other than that of the Prophet's (صَلَّى ٱللَّهُ عَلَيْهِ وَعَلَىٰ آلِهِ وَسَلَّمَ) is more complete than his guidance and that someone else's judgement is better than his judgement, such as those who prefer the judgement of the false deities over his judgement, then he is a disbeliever.[1]

[1] Included in this is those who believe that the laws of Islām are not suitable for the present time and they are only ancient laws. Also those who believe that man-made laws are equal to or better than the laws and legislation of Islām.

Fifth: Whoever hates something that the Messenger (صَلَّى اللَّهُ عَلَيْهِ وَعَلَى آلِهِ وَسَلَّمَ) came with, even though he may act on it, has disbelieved.[1]

Sixth: Whoever mocks or ridicules any part of the Messenger's Religion or its rewards or punishments has committed an act of disbelief.[2]

The proof for this is the saying of Allāh:

﴿قُلْ أَبِاللَّهِ وَءَايَٰتِهِۦ وَرَسُولِهِۦ كُنتُمْ تَسْتَهْزِءُونَ ٦٥ لَا تَعْتَذِرُوا۟ قَدْ كَفَرْتُم بَعْدَ إِيمَٰنِكُمْ﴾

> **"Say: Was it Allāh and His verses and His Messenger that you were mocking? Make no excuses, you have disbelieved after having had belief."** [*al-Tawbah* 9:65-66]

Seventh: Magic, and from that are the types that causes a person to love what he does not desire, or turns a person away from what they do desire. So whoever performs that or is pleased with it being done, has committed disbelief.[3]

The proof for this is the saying of Allāh:

---

[1] An example of this is those who hate plural marriage in Islām, even though they may accept it.

[2] An example of this is those who mock the Muslim man who grows the beard or raises his pants above the ankles, or those who mock the *Ḥijāb* of the Muslim women.

[3] Based upon this a Muslim does not read horoscopes, does not go to fortune tellers, palm readers, or others who practice magic or claim knowledge of the unseen. Also, a Muslim does not look at or watch magic shows, or movies that contain magic such as Harry Potter and what is similar to that.

﴿وَمَا يُعَلِّمَانِ مِنْ أَحَدٍ حَتَّىٰ يَقُولَآ إِنَّمَا نَحْنُ فِتْنَةٌ فَلَا تَكْفُرْ﴾

"And neither of these two (angels) taught anyone (magic) until they first said to them: We are only a trial, so do not commit disbelief (by learning magic from us)." [*al-Baqarah* 2:102]

Eighth: Supporting and assisting the polytheists against the Muslims.

The proof for this is the saying of Allāh:

﴿وَمَن يَتَوَلَّهُم مِّنكُمْ فَإِنَّهُۥ مِنْهُمْ ۗ إِنَّ ٱللَّهَ لَا يَهْدِى ٱلْقَوْمَ ٱلظَّـٰلِمِينَ﴾

"And whoever amongst you takes them (i.e. the disbelievers) as allies and protectors then he is indeed from among them. Verily, Allāh does not guide a wrong doing people."

[*al-Mā'idah* 5:51]

Ninth: Whoever believes that it is permitted for some people to exit outside what has been legislated upon Muḥammad (صَلَّىٰ ٱللَّٰهُ عَلَيْهِ وَسَلَّمَ), just as Khaḍr[1] was allowed to exit outside the legislation of Mūsā (عَلَيْهِ ٱلسَّلَامُ) then he is a disbeliever.[2]

---

[1] Some scholars say that Khadr was a righteous man and some have said he was a Prophet.

[2] An example of this is a misguided sect that ascribes to Islām known as *Ṣūfis*. Some extreme ones from among them claim that they have reached a level where all obligations such as prayer and fasting have been lifted from them and they are excused from doing acts of worship.

Tenth: Turning away from Allāh's Religion, not learning it or implementing it.

The proof for this is the saying of Allāh:

﴿وَمَنْ أَظْلَمُ مِمَّن ذُكِّرَ بِـَٔايَٰتِ رَبِّهِۦ ثُمَّ أَعْرَضَ عَنْهَآ ۚ إِنَّا مِنَ ٱلْمُجْرِمِينَ مُنتَقِمُونَ ﴿٢٢﴾﴾

"And who does more wrong than he who is reminded of the signs of his Lord, then turns away from them. Verily, We shall exact retribution from the criminals." [*al-Sajdah* 32:22]

There is no difference with regard to (committing any of) these nullifiers, between the one who does it jokingly, the one who is serious, or the one who does so out of fear, save the one who is forced and coerced. All of these matters are from the gravest in danger and from those that are most prevalent, so the Muslim must beware of them and fear for himself from having these befall him. We seek refuge with Allāh from the things that earn His anger and His painful torment.

Chapter Thirteen
Ṭahārah (Purification)

The Prophet (صَلَّى ٱللَّهُ عَلَيْهِ وَسَلَّمَ) said:

"The key to the prayer is purification."

Purification is of two types. The first is spiritual purification which means that one purifies him or herself from *shirk* and all remnants of sin and disobedience to Allāh, and this is by remaining upon pure *Tawḥīd* and also turning to Allāh with sincere repentance from all sins.

The second type of purification is that which we would like to discuss in this chapter, which is physical purification. Physical purification must be performed if one falls into any ritual impurities.

The ritual impurities are of two types; major ritual impurity and for this one needs to perform *ghusl*, and the second is minor ritual impurity by which one needs to perform *Wuḍū'*. All ritual impurities must be lifted in order to perform the obligatory and voluntary prayers.

Allāh said:

﴿وَإِن كُنتُمْ جُنُبًا فَٱطَّهَّرُوا۟﴾

"If you are in the state of sexual impurity (janābah) then purify yourselves." [*Al-Mā'idah* 5:6]

Prophet Muḥammad said, "Allāh will not accept the prayer of one you if he falls into *ḥadath* (i.e. ritual impurity) until they perform *Wuḍū'*." Collected by Bukhārī and Muslim.

Chapter Fourteen
Pure Water, Etiquettes of Relieving Oneself, and Removing Any Barriers that Prevent the Water from Reaching the Skin

Water used for making *Wuḍūʿ* and *ghusl* must be water that is pure and purifying. What is meant is the water that is in the original state in which Allāh created it, such as water from rain, lakes, springs, rivers, or oceans. Water which comes from the tap inside homes is pure water because that normally comes from a source of pure water.

Water only becomes impure if its color, taste or smell changes with something that is impure, such as urine or the likes. If its color changes by something which is pure and it still can be called water, then that water still can be used. An example is if a bar of soap falls into the water and you take it out.

The water may change color slightly, but it changes with something which is pure in itself, so that water still can be used. If it changes with something pure up until the point that it can no longer be called water, it cannot be used for ritual purification. An example is if one places tea bags in water until it changes the color and taste. It is still pure in the sense that it is not considered to be an impurity, but it loses the property of being purifying.

This would be then called tea. Although it can be drank and is not considered to be impure, it cannot be used for *Wuḍūʿ* or *ghusl*, because it no longer retains the name of water.

What has preceded shows the great importance of the prayer in Islām, whereas it cannot be accepted unless one is purified with both spiritual purity which is *Tawḥīd*, and physical purity which is by using pure water.

Also, before one performs *Wuḍū'* they must have had performed *istinjā* or *istijmār*. This means that after one uses the bathroom from urination or defecation, one must follow that up with using water to purify themselves. This is called *istinjā*. Also one can perform *istijmār* after using the bathroom which is to clean oneself with pure stones or whatever takes its place.

Using clean toilet paper is acceptable. It is best to gather between water and stones/toilet paper for a more complete cleaning, but if one suffices with just water or just stones/toilet paper, this is sufficient. *Istinjā* and *istijmār* are both done with the left hand, not the right.

Leaving off purifying yourself after urination could be a reason for Allāh to punish you in your grave. It has been narrated that the Prophet Muḥammad (صَلَّى ٱللَّهُ عَلَيْهِ وَسَلَّمَ) passed by two graves and said:

> "Verily, these two are being punished, and they are not being punished regarding something that was difficult to leave off; as for one of them, then he used to tale-carry among the people, and as for the other, he did not use to guard himself from his urine."

Collected by Bukhārī and Muslim.

Also, if one uses the bathroom whilst outside, they should be sure to hide themselves from the eyes of the people, and they should not use the bathroom whilst facing the direction of the *qiblah* (i.e.

Makkah). A Muslim further does not use the bathroom upon a path where people walk, nor where people use for shade, such as under trees, nor where the people take water from such as fountains and its likes.
A proof for making the *istinjā*:

Anas ibn Malik reported:

> "The Prophet (صَلَّى ٱللَّهُ عَلَيْهِ وَعَلَىٰ آلِهِ وَسَلَّمَ) would go use the bathroom, so another young boy and I would carry a container of water and a small spear, and he would cleanse himself with the water."

Reported by Bukhārī and Muslim.

Also before performing *Wuḍū'*, one must be sure there is nothing that prevents the water from directly reaching the skin, such as clay, dough, paint and the likes. If something changes the skin color but does not place a barrier between the skin and water, like henna, then there's nothing wrong with that.

Lastly, if one has incontinence where one cannot control their bladder, flatulence where one has uncontrollable gas, or a woman continues bleeding outside her normal menstrual cycle, this is known as continuous impurity.

Each of them must wait until the time for prayer comes in and then perform *Wuḍū'* and pray. Whatever impurities comes from them after the *Wuḍū'* is excused. They do this for each prayer.

Chapter Fifteen
Wuḍū‘ [Ritual Ablution]

It is obligatory for the one who wants to perform any prayer to perform *Wuḍū‘* with water.

[Proof]:

Allāh says:

﴿يَٰٓأَيُّهَا ٱلَّذِينَ ءَامَنُوٓاْ إِذَا قُمۡتُمۡ إِلَى ٱلصَّلَوٰةِ فَٱغۡسِلُواْ وُجُوهَكُمۡ وَأَيۡدِيَكُمۡ إِلَى ٱلۡمَرَافِقِ وَٱمۡسَحُواْ بِرُءُوسِكُمۡ وَأَرۡجُلَكُمۡ إِلَى ٱلۡكَعۡبَيۡنِۚ﴾

> **"O you who believe, when you stand for the prayer then wash your faces, then your hands up until the elbows, then wipe over your head, and (wash) your feet up to the ankles…"** [*al-Ma'idah* 5:6]

Also, the Prophet (صَلَّىٱللَّهُعَلَيْهِوَعَلَىٰآلِهِوَسَلَّمَ) said:

> "Allāh does not accept the prayer without purification."

The description of the *Wuḍū‘* that Prophet Muḥammad (صَلَّىٱللَّهُعَلَيْهِوَعَلَىٰآلِهِوَسَلَّمَ) would make comes in the following *ḥadīth*:

[Proof]:

Ḥumrān, the freed slave of ʿUthmān Ibn ʿAffān said that he saw ʿUthmān (رَضِيَ اللَّهُ عَنْهُ) call for a vessel with water. So he pulled water from the vessel onto his two hands and washed them three times. Then he placed his right hand in the vessel and placed water in his mouth and rinsed it around and also up his nose and then blew it out of his nose. Then he washed his face three times and then his hands up to the elbows three times. Then he wiped over his head and then washed both of his feet three times. Then he said: 'I saw the Prophet (صَلَّى اللَّهُ عَلَيْهِ وَعَلَى آلِهِ وَسَلَّمَ) make a *Wuḍūʿ* just like this *Wuḍūʿ* of mine..."

Reported by Bukhārī and Muslim.

This *ḥadīth* clarifies that these are the steps to performing a correct and complete *Wuḍūʿ*:

One first begins by saying *Bismillāh* (i.e. in the Name of Allāh)

1- Wash the hands three times beginning with the right hand, then the left hand.

2- Place water in the mouth and nose, using the right hand, with one scoop of water for both. Rinse out your mouth and then blow the water from the nose three times, using the left hand.

3- Wash the entire face three times. The beard is included in the washing of the face, so one washes the beard along with it, even if it is long.

4- Wash the arms [starting from the tips of the fingers] up to the elbows three times, beginning with the right arm, then the left arm.

5- Wipe over the head from front to back and then back to front. Then place the forefingers in the ears (without getting new water) and wipe the inside, and wipe the outside of the ears using the thumb. This is done one time.

6- Wash the feet up to the ankles three times, beginning with the right foot, and then the left foot.

O Muslim, be sure to make a full and complete *Wuḍū'*, having the water fully cover all the required limbs of *Wuḍū'*, giving particular attention to properly washing the feet.

The Prophet (صَلَّى ٱللَّهُ عَلَيْهِ وَعَلَىٰ آلِهِ وَسَلَّمَ) saw a man who was praying and had a spot on his foot the size of a coin, which he did not cover with water, so he commanded him to repeat the *Wuḍū'* and repeat the prayer.[1]

Making a full and complete *Wuḍū'* does not mean that one is wasteful with water, as this is something that has been prohibited. Rather, it means that each limb of *Wuḍū'* is properly and fully washed.

One of the companions asked the Prophet (صَلَّى ٱللَّهُ عَلَيْهِ وَسَلَّمَ),

> "Could there be wastefulness (with water) even while making *Wuḍū'*? He responded? "Yes, even if you are at a flowing river[2]."

[1] Collected by Aḥmad (3/424) and Abū Dāwud (175)

[2] Collected by Aḥmad (2/221) and Ibn Mājah (425).

Chapter Sixteen
Wiping Over the Khuffs [Leather Socks]

The religion of Islām is not a religion of hardship, rather it is a religion of ease. From the examples of this ease is that Allāh has allowed the wiping over the two *khuffs* (leather socks), or that which takes that ruling such as cotton or wool socks and the likes.

Some of the scholars of Islām have reported a consensus regarding the permissibility of wiping over the *khuffs*. The following are the conditions for wiping over the two *khuffs* or socks:

(1) That the *khuffs* or socks are worn while the feet are pure after a full *Wuḍū'* from washing.

(2) That the *khuffs* or socks be wiped over during the prescribed period which is one day for the resident (24 hours), and three days for the traveler (72 hours). The period of wiping begins after the first time a person wipes over the *khuffs*, not when a person first wears the *khuffs* or socks, and Allāh knows best.

(3) That the *khuffs* or socks be wiped over as a result of minor impurity and not from what necessitates major impurity. (This will come in the next chapter)

What nullifies the wiping over the *khuffs* or socks is:

(1) If a person falls into major impurity and has to make a *ghusl*.

(2) If the time period of the wiping is up, then a person must take the socks off and wash the feet when making their next *Wuḍū'*.

Important: Only the top of the *khuffs* or socks are wiped, not the bottom. The benefit we get from this is that the religion is not understood by intellect, rather it is based upon following the text of the *Qur'ān* and *Sunnah.*

The companion 'Alī Ibn Abū Ṭālib (رَضِيَ ٱللَّهُ عَنْهُ) said:

> "If the religion was based upon opinion, the bottom of the *khuffs* would have been wiped over instead of the top, and indeed I saw the Messenger of Allāh (صَلَّى ٱللَّهُ عَلَيْهِ وَعَلَىٰ آلِهِ وَسَلَّمَ) wipe over the top of his *khuffs*[1]."

If one removes what he wears over the sock several times such as shoes or boots, there is no harm in that if he already began wiping over the socks.

Taking off the socks in itself does not nullify the *Wuḍū'* according to the correct position.

---

[1] Reported by Abū Dāwūd (no. 162) and declared *Ṣaḥīḥ* by *Shaykh* al-Albānī.

Chapter Seventeen
What Nullifies the Wuḍū'

That which nullifies the *Wuḍū'* is anything that comes from the two private parts such as urine, stools, semen from ejaculation, pre-seminal fluid, and passing wind. Also losing consciousness by way of deep sleep, being intoxicated or insanity breaks the *Wuḍū'*, because it is possible that something came from the private parts and they did not realize it.

Also what nullifies the *Wuḍū'* is touching the private part with sexual desire, eating camel's meat, and apostasy from *Islām* (may Allāh protect us from that). Blood from nosebleeds and bleeding from the gums or the likes does not invalidate the *Wuḍū'*.

O Muslim, what you must know is that *shayṭān* (i.e. the devil) is very diligent in corrupting the worship of mankind so they can be like him amongst the losers, and far away from the mercy of Allāh. He sometimes whispers to a person that they did not perform *Wuḍū'* correctly, or that they nullified their *Wuḍū'*, when in reality that is not the case. In this case, the fundamental principle is "Certainty is not removed by doubt."

Meaning, if you are certain that the last thing you remember was that you were in the state of *Wuḍū'* and you have doubt whether you nullified it or not, you cast aside that doubt and remain upon certainty, which is that you are in *Wuḍū'*. The opposite is also true. If you were certain that the last thing you did was nullify your *Wuḍū'* and you have doubt as to whether you performed a new *Wuḍū'* or not, again you base it upon what you are certain of which is that you are not in *Wuḍū'*.

So this is an important principle that covers many matters of the religion: Things remain upon their origin until one has certainty of its opposite.

Chapter Eighteen
What Constitutes the Ghusl [Ritual Washing of the Entire Body]

You have already learned that there are two types of impurities: minor impurity and major impurity. Minor impurity is lifted by performing *Wuḍū'*, which is obligatory for your prayer to be accepted. In this chapter we will discuss what constitutes a major impurity and how to lift this impurity. The following necessitates that one makes a *ghusl*:

1-That a man or woman ejaculates because of sexual desire, and this includes if one is awake or asleep (i.e. a wet dream[1]).

2- Sexual intercourse. If the man penetrates the woman to the extent that the tip of the penis disappears into the vagina, then *ghusl* is obligatory upon both of them, even if they do not ejaculate.

Proof:

The Prophet (صَلَّى ٱللَّهُ عَلَيْهِ وَسَلَّمَ) said: "If the two circumcised parts meet, then *ghusl* becomes obligatory."

3- If the woman has her menstrual cycle (i.e. period), then she must make *ghusl* once her cycle is over and before she prays. Likewise, the woman must make a *ghusl* when she finishes her post-natal bleeding.

4-Death. If a Muslim dies, he or she must be given a *ghusl*, as this is what the Prophet (صَلَّى ٱللَّهُ عَلَيْهِ وَسَلَّمَ) commanded.

---

[1] If a person remembers a sexual dream but does not see any wetness, they do not have to make the *ghusl*.

5- If the disbeliever embraces *Islām* then he should make a *ghusl*.

All the above are *ghusls* which are obligatory. There are also times when *ghusl* is recommended, such as on Friday for the *Jumu'ah* prayer.

Chapter Nineteen
A Description of the Ghusl

There are two descriptions of the *ghusl*: one that is recommended and more complete and one that is a lesser *ghusl* yet accepted if one does it. The complete *ghusl* has come in two *ḥadīths* narrated by two of the wives of the Messenger of Allāh (صَلَّى ٱللَّهُ عَلَيْهِ وَسَلَّمَ), and it can be done in two ways:

The [complete] recommended type of *ghusl*:

[Proofs]:

> Narrated ʿĀʾishah (رَضِيَ ٱللَّهُ عَنْهَا) that if the Messenger of Allāh (صَلَّى ٱللَّهُ عَلَيْهِ وَسَلَّمَ) made a *ghusl* from *janābah*[1] he would first wash his two hands, then he would perform *Wuḍūʿ* as he would do for the prayer. Then he would wash his whole body. He would then use his hands to comb through his hair until the point he was sure that he washed it thoroughly to the scalp. He would pour water over it (i.e. his head) three times. Then he would wash the rest of his body."

Reported by Bukhārī and Muslim.

Narrated Maymūnah bint al Ḥārith, wife of the Messenger of Allāh (صَلَّى ٱللَّهُ عَلَيْهِ وَسَلَّمَ) that she said:

> "I prepared for the Messenger of Allāh (صَلَّى ٱللَّهُ عَلَيْهِ وَسَلَّمَ) his water to make *ghusl* from *janābah*. He poured water with his right

---

[1] The state of sexual impurity.

hand over his left two or three times, then he washed his private part. Then he hit his hand on the floor or on the wall two or three times. Then he gargled water in his mouth and sniffed it up his nose. Then he washed his face and two arms. Then he poured water over his head and then washed his body. Then he moved to another place and washed his feet..."

Reported by Bukhārī and Muslim.

The lesser *ghusl*:

The lesser type of *ghusl* is that one pours water over their entire body with the intention of lifting the major impurity. So if one has a wet dream for example, and gets in the shower and lets the water touch his entire body and he or she intends to remove the major impurity, then this is sufficient.

If a woman is performing *ghusl* from her menstrual cycle and her hair is braided, she must take out her braids.

Chapter Twenty
Tayammum

In the event that water is unavailable or it is available but a person cannot use it because of its scarcity and the need to drink it, or a person cannot use it due to an Islāmic excuse such as sickness, and using the water will increase that sickness or delay one's healing, or if one fears the extreme cold and there is no way to heat the water, then it is legislated to perform *tayammum*.

Allāh says in the *Qur'ān*,

﴿وَإِن كُنتُم مَّرْضَىٰٓ أَوْ عَلَىٰ سَفَرٍ أَوْ جَآءَ أَحَدٌ مِّنكُم مِّنَ ٱلْغَآئِطِ أَوْ لَٰمَسْتُمُ
ٱلنِّسَآءَ فَلَمْ تَجِدُوا۟ مَآءً فَتَيَمَّمُوا۟ صَعِيدًا طَيِّبًا فَٱمْسَحُوا۟
بِوُجُوهِكُمْ وَأَيْدِيكُم مِّنْهُ﴾

> **"But if you are ill or on a journey and any of you have come from answering the call of nature, or if you have been in contact with women (i.e. sexual intercourse) and you cannot find water then perform tayammum with clean earth and rub therewith your faces and hands."** [*al-Mā'idah* 5:6]

One may use for *tayammum* anything on the earth such as dirt, sand, and the likes.

The description of *tayammum*: A person strikes the earth with his two hands then wipes over his face and wipes his two hands.

Tayammum is nullified by that which nullifies *Wuḍū'* and by whatever necessitates *ghusl*. *Tayammum* is also nullified when water becomes available if one made *tayammum* because of absence of water, or whenever one's excuse ceases, which allowed *tayammum* to be performed, such as sickness or other than that.

Chapter Twenty One
The Conditions that Must Precede the Prayer

There are nine conditions that the scholars mention that must be fulfilled before one makes the prayer:

(1) One must be a Muslim, so the prayer is not accepted from the disbeliever because of his or her disbelief.

(2) One must be of sound intellect. The pen is lifted from the one who is insane.

(3) One must be of age of discernment, which is nine years of age.

(4) One must be in the state of *Wuḍūʿ*.

(5) Impurities must be lifted from one's body, clothing, and place of prayer.

(6) One's *ʿawrah* (private area) must be covered. For the men the private area is between the naval and knee, and the whole of the Muslim woman is an *ʿawrah*.

(7) One must face the *qiblah*. This is the direction of Makkah which is roughly Northeast from where we are in the United States.

(8) The time for the prayer must have entered. One cannot make the prayer except in its prescribed time.

(9) One must have an intention. The Prophet (صَلَّى ٱللَّهُ عَلَيْهِ وَسَلَّمَ) said: "Actions are only by intentions."

Chapter Twenty Two
Brief Description of the Prayer of the Prophet (ﷺ)

The Prophet (صَلَّى ٱللَّهُ عَلَيْهِ وَسَلَّمَ) said:

"Pray as you have seen me pray."

Collected by Bukhārī and Muslim.

As you have already learned, the prayer has a major status in the Religion of Islām. It is the second most important pillar of Islām, it distinguishes the believer from the disbeliever, and it is the first thing that the servant will be asked about on the Day of Resurrection.

Additionally, what shows its importance is that Allāh legislated the prayer on the night that the Prophet made the night journey and ascension to the heavens whereas all other acts of worship were legislated through the Angel Jibrīl coming to the Prophet (صَلَّى ٱللَّهُ عَلَيْهِ وَسَلَّمَ) with revelation.

The prayer consists of pillars, obligations and recommended matters. These pillars must be accomplished, and without them the prayer is invalid. The obligations also cannot be left off, but if one forgets them they can be remedied by two supplemental prostrations at the end of the prayer, known as prostration for forgetfulness.

We will point out the pillars and obligations as we describe the prayer of the Messenger of Allāh (صَلَّى ٱللَّهُ عَلَيْهِ وَسَلَّمَ).

The Prophet's Prayer (صَلَّى ٱللَّهُ عَلَيْهِ وَسَلَّمَ)

The Prophet (صَلَّى ٱللَّهُ عَلَيْهِ وَسَلَّمَ) would stand for the prayer (pillar 1), facing the direction of the *qiblah* and raise his two hands to the level of the two shoulders or earlobes, with the inner side of his fingers facing the *qiblah* and would say *Allāhu Akbar* (pillar 2)[1].

He would then place his right hand over his left hand or left arm and put them on his chest.

He would then mention the opening glorification and then seek refuge with Allāh from the *shayṭān* (i.e. the devil), and then say *Bismillahir Raḥmānir Raḥīm.*

Then he would recite the *Fātiḥah*[2] (pillar 3), and when he was finished reciting it he would say "*Āmīn*[3]".

After that he would recite a *sūrah* from the *Qur'ān.*

Afterwards he would raise his hands just has he did in the very beginning and say *Allāhu Akbar*[4] (obligation1), and then he would go into the bowing position [*Rukū'*] (pillar 4).

---

[1] It is a must that one says this very initial saying of *Allāhu Akbar* for their prayer to commence. If one leaves it off or forgets it, their prayer does not begin.

[2] The *Fātiḥah* is the greatest *Sūrah* in the *Qur'ān* and the prayer is not valid if one does not recite it. We will include the *Fātiḥah*, the opening glorification, seeking refuge from the devil, the *Tashahhud* and the Salutations upon the Prophet at the end of this chapter.

[3] Meaning, answer O Allāh.

[4] All the sayings of *Allāhu Akbar* throughout the prayer besides the initial saying are obligations and not pillars.

He would place his two hands on his two knees with the fingers spread out.

He would make his back straight and line his head with his back. He wouldn't raise his head too much, nor droop his head. In this position he would say *Subḥāna Rabbiyal Aẓīm*[1] (obligation 2).

He then would raise his head from bowing (pillar 5) saying: *Samiʿ Allāhu Liman Ḥamidah*[2] (obligation 3), raising his two hands as he did going into bowing.

When he stood up straight he said: *Rabanā Laka al-Ḥamd*[3] (obligation 4).[4]

Then he would say *Allāhu Akbar* and fall into prostration [5][*Sujūd*] (pillar 6).

He would prostrate on seven limbs which are the forehead including the nose, the two hands, the two knees, and the tips of the toes of the two feet[6]. The toes of the feet should face the direction of the *qiblah*. One's elbows should not be spread flat on the ground as an animal lays. He would say during this prostration *Subḥāna Rabbiyal Aʿlā*[7] (obligation 5).

---

[1] Glorified is Allah the Most Great.

[2] Allah answers those who praise Him.

[3] Our Lord, and all praise is for You.

[4] During this standing one may place their hands back on their chest or leave them to their side. This is not an issue where the scholars would differ to the point that they would argue or boycott one another.

[5] When going into prostration and saying *Allāhu Akbar*, one may raise their hands sometimes, not all the time.

[6] In prostration, the two feet should be joined together and not spread apart.

[7] Glorified is Allah, the Most High.

He then would raise his head from prostration (pillar 7) and say *Allāhu Akbar*[1].

He would spread out his left foot and sit his bottom on it and prop up his right foot and place his two hands on his two thighs (pillar 8).

Then he would say *Rabbī ighfirlī, Rabbī ighfirlī*[2] (obligation 6).

Then he would say *Allāhu Akbar* and prostrate for a second time in the manner he did in the first.

Then he raised his head again saying *Allāhu Akbar* and returned back to the standing position, taking a brief sitting before he stood back up.

With this one has completed one *rakʿah*, and does in the second *rakʿah* exactly what he did in the first.

When one rises from the second prostration in the second *rakʿah*, he sits (obligation 7) for the first *tashahhud*. He sits just as he sat between the two prostrations, spreading out his left foot and sitting his bottom on it, and propping up the right foot and placing the two hands on the thighs.

After that he makes a fist with his right hand on his thigh and then extends his pointer finger while looking at it and recites the *tashahhud* (obligation 8).

---

[1] Here one does not raise the hands except occasionally.

[2] O my Lord forgive me, O my Lord forgive me.

When he finishes reciting the *tashahhud*, he stands for the third and fourth rak'ah[1]. In these rak'ah's one only recites the *Fātiḥah* and does not recite a surah after it.

During the final sitting, one sits (pillar 9) for the last *tashahhud* in the *tawwaruk* position[2] and recites the final *tashahhud* (pillar 10)[3].

After that he sends salutations upon the Prophet (صَلَّى ٱللَّهُ عَلَيْهِ وَسَلَّمَ) (pillar 11).

Afterwards one seeks refuge from the punishment of the grave, the punishment of the Hellfire, from the trials of living and death, and from the trials of the *dajjāl* (i.e. anti-christ).

Lastly one turns his head to the right and says *Al-Salāmu 'Alaykum Wa Raḥmatullāh* (pillar 12) and does the same to the left.

There are two more important pillars in the prayer which is that one must keep the sequential order of the prayer (pillar 13), and that one must have tranquility in all the positions of the prayer (pillar 14).

That means that all limbs must come to a rest in each position before going to the next position.

These make the pillars of the prayer 14 and the obligations 8. There are many recommended *Sunnah* acts of the prayer which you will learn as you further your studies, if Allāh wills.

---

[1] Every prayer does not consist of four *rak'ahs*. The *fajr* prayer is two *rak'ahs*, the *Ẓuhr* and *'Aṣr* prayer are four *rak'ahs*, the *Maghrib* prayer is three *rak'ahs*, and the *'Ishā'* prayer is four *rak'ahs*.

[2] See "A Simple Description of the Prophet's Prayer for Beginners with Illustrations" (point 71) by Abu Khadijah.

[3] Which is the same wording as the first *tashahhud*.

O Muslim, this is a brief description of the Prophet's prayer as it has been reported in the legislated text. Upon you is to give great importance to your prayer, and that it be in accordance to the prayer of the Prophet (صَلَّىٱللَّهُعَلَيْهِوَسَلَّمَ).

The Fātiḥah, Opening Glorification, Tashahhud, and Salutations Upon the Prophet (ﷺ)

Important Note: The prayer must be said in the Arabic language, and reading Arabic transliteration can never suffice for the original Arabic text, as there are letters in the Arabic language that do not have an English equivalent. Having said this, we encourage the new Muslim to hasten to enroll in a class where they can learn how to read the Arabic language, which is the language of the *Qur'ān*, and our Prophet Muḥammad (ﷺ). The following is a *fatwā* (religious verdict) regarding praying in other than the Arabic language.

The permanent committee of scholars in Saudi Arabia were asked the following question[1]:

[Q]: Can the prayer be said in other than the Arabic language?

[A]: The prayer cannot be said in other than the Arabic language whilst one has the ability (to utilize it). Therefore, it is incumbent upon the Muslim to learn in the Arabic language (the matters of) the religion which are not permissible to be ignorant of. From that is learning the *Fātiḥah*, the *tashahhud*, the *tasmī*[2]', the *taḥmīd*[3], and the *tasbīḥ*[4] in *rukū'* and *sujūd*. Likewise, saying *rabbī ighfirlī*[5] between the two prostrations, and the *taslīm*[6]. As for the one who in incapable of

[1] *Fatwā* no. 4211. Volume 6 page 405.

[2] Saying *Sami' Allāhu Liman Ḥamidah.*

[3] Saying *Alḥamdulillah*

[4] Saying *Subḥāna Rabbiyal A'lā* and *Subḥāna Rabbiyal 'Aẓīm*

[5] i.e. Lord, forgive me.

[6] Saying *Al-Salāmu 'Alaykum Wa Raḥmatullāh*

utilizing the Arabic language, then upon him (or her) is to say those matters in their language, except the *Fātiḥah*; this is because to recite it in other than the Arabic language is incorrect, and the same goes for other (*sūrahs*) of the *Qur'ān*. Upon him (i.e. the one incapable) is to say in its place the *tasbīḥ*, the *taḥmīd*, the *tahlīl*[1], and the *takbīr*[2]. This is due to the *ḥadīth* of 'Abdullāh Ibn Abū Awfā (رَضِيَ ٱللَّهُ عَنْهُ) that he said: 'A man came to the Prophet (صَلَّى ٱللَّهُ عَلَيْهِ وَسَلَّمَ) and said: I am unable to take (memorize) anything from the *Qur'ān*, so teach me what will suffice me on its behalf? He (the Prophet) said: Say *Subḥān Allāh, Alḥamdulilah, Lā ilāha illā Allāh, Allāhu Akbar*, and *Lā Ḥawla wa Lā Quwwata illā billāh al-'Alī al-'Aẓīm*." The *ḥadīth* was collected by Aḥmad, Abū Dāwūd, Al-Nisā'ī, Ibn Ḥibbān, al-Dāraquṭnī, and al-Ḥākim. Also due to the statement of Allāh the Glorified and Most High: 'Fear Allāh as far as you are able', and the statement of the Prophet (صَلَّى ٱللَّهُ عَلَيْهِ وَسَلَّمَ):

'If I command you with a matter, then do it as far as you are able', until one is able to learn the Arabic language, and one should hasten to do so."

Opening Glorification:

سُبْحَانَكَ اللَّهُمَّ وَبِحَمْدِكَ، وَتَبَارَكَ اسْمُكَ، وَتَعَالَى جَدُّكَ، وَلَا إِلَهَ غَيْرُكَ

You are Glorified, O Allāh and Praised; Your Name is Blessed, Your Majesty is Exalted, and none has the right to be worshipped (in truth) but You.

---

[1] Saying *Lā ilāha illā Allāh*

[2] Saying *Allāhu Akbar*

Seeking refuge from *shayṭān* before recitation

أَعُوذُ بِٱللَّهِ مِنَ ٱلشَّيْطَٰنِ ٱلرَّجِيمِ

I seek refuge with Allāh from the accursed devil (distant from Allāh's mercy).

Or one may say

أَعُوذُ بِاللَّهِ السَّمِيعِ الْعَلِيمِ مِنَ الشَّيْطَانِ الرَّجِيمِ مِنْ هَمْزِهِ وَنَفْخِهِ وَنَفْثِهِ

I seek refuge with Allāh from the accursed devil (distant from Allāh's mercy), (and) from his madness, his arrogance, and his evil poetry.

Sūrah al Fātiḥah

﴿بِسْمِ ٱللَّهِ ٱلرَّحْمَٰنِ ٱلرَّحِيمِ ۝١ ٱلْحَمْدُ لِلَّهِ رَبِّ ٱلْعَٰلَمِينَ ۝٢ ٱلرَّحْمَٰنِ ٱلرَّحِيمِ ۝٣ مَٰلِكِ يَوْمِ
ٱلدِّينِ ۝٤ إِيَّاكَ نَعْبُدُ وَإِيَّاكَ نَسْتَعِينُ ۝٥ ٱهْدِنَا ٱلصِّرَٰطَ ٱلْمُسْتَقِيمَ ۝٦ صِرَٰطَ ٱلَّذِينَ أَنْعَمْتَ
عَلَيْهِمْ غَيْرِ ٱلْمَغْضُوبِ عَلَيْهِمْ وَلَا ٱلضَّآلِّينَ ۝٧﴾

In the Name of Allāh, the Most Merciful, the Bestower of Mercy
All praise and thanks are Allāh's, the Lord of mankind, jinn and all creation.
The Most Gracious, the Most Merciful
The Only Owner of the Day of Recompense
You (Alone) we worship, and You (Alone) we ask for help.

Guide us to the straight way.[1]
The way of those on whom you have bestowed Your Grace, not (the way) of those who earned Your anger, nor of those who went astray.

The *Tashahhud*

التَّحِيَّاتُ لِلَّهِ، وَالصَّلَوَاتُ، وَالطَّيِّبَاتُ، السَّلَامُ عَلَى النَّبِيِّ وَرَحْمَةُ اللهِ وَبَرَكَاتُهُ، السَّلَامُ عَلَيْنَا وَعَلَى عِبَادِ اللهِ الصَّالِحِينَ، أَشْهَدُ أَنْ لَا إِلَهَ إِلَّا اللهُ، وَأَشْهَدُ أَنَّ مُحَمَّدًا عَبْدُهُ وَرَسُولُهُ

All exaltations, all supplications and good words are due to Allāh. May peace be on the Prophet, and also the Mercy of Allāh and His Blessings. May peace be upon us, and all the righteous slaves of Allāh. I bear witness that none has the right to be worshipped (in truth) except Allāh, and I bear witness that Muḥammad is His slave and messenger.

[1] It is important to learn this Sūrah from a qualified teacher, so that you are able to recite it properly, as the correct recitation of Fātiḥah is required for your prayer.

We advise the brothers and sisters to learn to read the Qur'ān in the correct manner by learning the Arabic alphabet from a qualified teacher and then the vowels and so on.

This is because the lazy approach, which is to rely upon transliteration with English letters, inevitably leads to a person making major grammatical errors and mispronunciations when reading the Quran.

The Salāt upon the Prophet (ﷺ), or the Ibrāhīm Supplication

اللَّهُمَّ صَلِّ عَلَى مُحَمَّدٍ وَعَلَى آلِ مُحَمَّدٍ كَمَا صَلَّيْتَ عَلَى إِبْرَاهِيمَ وَآلِ إِبْرَاهِيمَ إِنَّكَ حَمِيدٌ مَجِيدٌ، وَبَارِكْ عَلَى مُحَمَّدٍ وَعَلَى آلِ مُحَمَّدٍ كَمَا بَارَكْتَ عَلَى إِبْرَاهِيمَ وَآلِ إِبْرَاهِيمَ إِنَّكَ حَمِيدٌ مَجِيدٌ

O Allāh, send prayers upon Muḥammad and on the family of Muḥammad, as you sent prayers on Ibrāhīm and on the family of Ibrāhīm; You are the One full of Praise, full of Glory. O Allāh, send blessings upon Muḥammad and on the family of Muḥammad, just as You sent blessings upon Ibrāhīm and on the family of Ibrāhīm; You are the One full of Praise, full of Glory.

Chapter Twenty-Three
Islām is One Path Not Many Paths

O Muslim, the path that leads to Allāh is one and not many. For this reason, Allāh has instructed His servants to supplicate to Him that He guides them to His straight path. Allāh says:

﴿ ٱهۡدِنَا ٱلصِّرَٰطَ ٱلۡمُسۡتَقِيمَ ۝٦ صِرَٰطَ ٱلَّذِينَ أَنۡعَمۡتَ عَلَيۡهِمۡ غَيۡرِ ٱلۡمَغۡضُوبِ عَلَيۡهِمۡ وَلَا ٱلضَّآلِّينَ ۝٧ ﴾

> **"Guide us to the straight path. The path of whom You bestowed Your blessings upon. Not the path of those whom incurred Your wrath, nor those who went astray."** [*al-Fatiḥah* 1:6-7]

Allāh also says:

﴿ فَإِمَّا يَأۡتِيَنَّكُم مِّنِّي هُدٗى فَمَنِ ٱتَّبَعَ هُدَايَ فَلَا يَضِلُّ وَلَا يَشۡقَىٰ ﴾

> **"Then if there comes to you guidance from Me, then whoever follows the guidance shall neither go astray nor fall into distress and misery."** [*Tā Ha* 20:123]

Ibn Abbās (رَضِيَ ٱللَّهُ عَنْهُمَا) stated about this verse, "He will not go astray in the worldly life, and will not be miserable in the hereafter."

Also, due to Allāh knowing that other paths would appear, He instructed His Messenger (صَلَّىٰ ٱللَّهُ عَلَيْهِ وَسَلَّمَ) to inform the people to follow His path alone, and not follow the other paths. Allāh said:

﴿وَأَنَّ هَٰذَا صِرَٰطِي مُسْتَقِيمًا فَٱتَّبِعُوهُ ۖ وَلَا تَتَّبِعُوا۟ ٱلسُّبُلَ فَتَفَرَّقَ
بِكُمْ عَن سَبِيلِهِۦ ۚ ذَٰلِكُمْ وَصَّىٰكُم بِهِۦ لَعَلَّكُمْ تَتَّقُونَ ﴿١٥٣﴾﴾

> **"And verily, this is my straight path so follow it, and do not follow the other paths, for they will separate you away from His path. This He has ordained for you that you may become from the pious."** [*Al-Anʿam* 6:153]

The Messenger of Allāh (صَلَّىٰ ٱللَّهُ عَلَيْهِ وَسَلَّمَ) drew with his hand a straight line in the earth and said, "This is the path of Allāh". Then he drew (lines) on the right of it and its left and said, "These are the other paths. There is not a path from them except there is a devil calling to it." Then he recited the above verse (in *Sūrah al-Anʿam*).

Ibn Abbās (رَضِيَ ٱللَّهُ عَنْهُمَا) said:

> "Allāh commanded the believers with clinging to the *Jamāʿah* (i.e. the group of the Muslims upon the truth), and He forbade them from dividing and separating. He also informed that those before them were only destroyed because of argumentation and disputing in the religion."

So with this it becomes clear that the path that leads to Allāh is one path, not many. Also there are paths that the devil calls to that are in opposition to the path of Allāh. These are paths of misguidance and deviation that are not based upon *Qurʿān* and *Sunnah*. The correct path that leads to Allāh is by remaining upon the guidance that Allāh sent down in the *Qur'ān* and what the Prophet (صَلَّى ٱللَّهُ عَلَيْهِ وَسَلَّمَ) came with in his *Sunnah*, as understood by his companions.

Chapter Twenty-Four
Division Among the Muslims and its Remedy

O Muslim! In the *Qur'ān*, Allāh has criticized division and separation and has commanded with unity. Allāh said:

﴿يَٰٓأَيُّهَا ٱلَّذِينَ ءَامَنُواْ ٱتَّقُواْ ٱللَّهَ حَقَّ تُقَاتِهِۦ وَلَا تَمُوتُنَّ إِلَّا وَأَنتُم
مُّسۡلِمُونَ ١٠٢ وَٱعۡتَصِمُواْ بِحَبۡلِ ٱللَّهِ جَمِيعٗا وَلَا تَفَرَّقُواْۚ وَٱذۡكُرُواْ
نِعۡمَتَ ٱللَّهِ عَلَيۡكُمۡ إِذۡ كُنتُمۡ أَعۡدَآءٗ فَأَلَّفَ بَيۡنَ قُلُوبِكُمۡ فَأَصۡبَحۡتُم
بِنِعۡمَتِهِۦٓ إِخۡوَٰنٗا وَكُنتُمۡ عَلَىٰ شَفَا حُفۡرَةٖ مِّنَ ٱلنَّارِ فَأَنقَذَكُم مِّنۡهَاۗ كَذَٰلِكَ
يُبَيِّنُ ٱللَّهُ لَكُمۡ ءَايَٰتِهِۦ لَعَلَّكُمۡ تَهۡتَدُونَ ١٠٣﴾

"O you who believe! Fear Allāh as He should be feared, and die not except in a state of Islām (as Muslims). And hold fast, all of you together, to the Rope of Allāh (i.e. this Qur'ān), and be not divided among yourselves, and remember Allāh's Favour on you, for you were enemies one to another but He joined your hearts together, so that, by His Grace, you became brethren (in Islāmic Faith), and you were on the brink of a pit of Fire, and He saved you from it. Thus Allāh makes His *Ayat* (proofs, evidences, verses, lessons, signs, revelations, etc.,) clear to you, that you may be guided." [*Āl-'Imrān* 3:103-104]

Allāh also said:

﴿وَأَطِيعُوا۟ ٱللَّهَ وَرَسُولَهُۥ وَلَا تَنَٰزَعُوا۟ فَتَفْشَلُوا۟ وَتَذْهَبَ رِيحُكُمْ ۖ وَٱصْبِرُوٓا۟ ۚ إِنَّ ٱللَّهَ مَعَ ٱلصَّٰبِرِينَ ﴿٤٦﴾﴾

"And obey Allāh and His Messenger, and do not dispute (with one another) lest you lose courage and your strength depart, and be patient. Surely, Allāh is with those who are al-Ṣābirīn (the patient ones, etc.)." [*al-Anfāl* 8:46]

Prophet Muḥammad (ﷺ) said:

> "Verily, Allāh loves for you three things and He hates for you three things; He loves that you worship Him and not associate any partners with Him, that you hold on together to the rope of Allāh and do not divide, and that you give sincere advice to those whom Allāh has placed as leaders over you."

Reported by Muslim in his *Ṣaḥīḥ*.

At the same time, Allāh and His Messenger informed that division will occur, in order to warn the Muslims from falling victim to that. Furthermore, Allāh decreed this division to occur out of His infinite wisdom, and so it will become clear who remains patient in the face of tests and trials and who will not. This is to distinguish the wicked from the good and the hypocrites from the believers.

Allāh said:

﴿ الٓمٓ ﴿١﴾ أَحَسِبَ ٱلنَّاسُ أَن يُتْرَكُوٓا۟ أَن يَقُولُوٓا۟ ءَامَنَّا وَهُمْ لَا يُفْتَنُونَ
﴿٢﴾ وَلَقَدْ فَتَنَّا ٱلَّذِينَ مِن قَبْلِهِمْ ۖ فَلَيَعْلَمَنَّ ٱللَّهُ ٱلَّذِينَ صَدَقُوا۟ وَلَيَعْلَمَنَّ
ٱلْكَٰذِبِينَ ﴿٣﴾ ﴾

> **"Alif-Lām-Mīm. Do people think that they will be left alone because they say: "We believe," and will not be tested. And We indeed tested those who were before them. And Allāh will certainly make (it) known (the truth of) those who are true, and will certainly make (it) known (the falsehood of) those who are liars."** [*al-ʿAnkabūt* 29:1-3]

The Prophet (صَلَّى ٱللَّٰهُ عَلَيْهِ وَسَلَّمَ) informed of these trials and spoke of its remedies. He (صَلَّى ٱللَّٰهُ عَلَيْهِ وَسَلَّمَ) said:

> "Whoever lives among you will see much differing, so upon you is to cling to my *Sunnah* and the *Sunnah* of the rightly guided caliphs after me. Bite down on that with your molar teeth, and beware of newly invented matters (in the religion) for every newly invented matter is misguidance."

And he said: "Indeed I am leaving you with two matters that if you hold onto, you will not go astray after me; the Book of Allāh and my *Sunnah*."

Also Allāh says:

﴿ يَٰٓأَيُّهَا ٱلَّذِينَ ءَامَنُوٓا۟ أَطِيعُوا۟ ٱللَّهَ وَأَطِيعُوا۟ ٱلرَّسُولَ وَأُو۟لِى ٱلْأَمْرِ مِنكُمْ ۖ فَإِن تَنَٰزَعْتُمْ فِى شَىْءٍ فَرُدُّوهُ إِلَى ٱللَّهِ وَٱلرَّسُولِ إِن كُنتُمْ تُؤْمِنُونَ بِٱللَّهِ وَٱلْيَوْمِ ٱلْءَاخِرِ ۚ ذَٰلِكَ خَيْرٌ وَأَحْسَنُ تَأْوِيلًا ﴿٥٩﴾ ﴾

"O you who believe! Obey Allāh and obey the Messenger (Muḥammad), and those of you (Muslims) who are in authority. (And) if you differ in anything amongst yourselves refer it to Allāh and His Messenger if you believe in Allāh and in the Last Day. That is better and more suitable for final determination." [*Al-Nisā'* 4:59]

So Allāh and His Messenger informed that when differing occurs one must return that differing back to Allāh and His messenger, and that is by referring all disputes back to the *Qur'ān*, and to the *Sunnah* of the Messenger of Allāh (ﷺ) for judgement.

When differing arises, the way of safety and salvation from that is to firmly cling to the *Sunnah* of the Messenger of Allāh and the *Sunnah* of his rightly guided caliphs, who were Abū Bakr, 'Umar, 'Uthmān and 'Alī (رَضِيَ ٱللَّهُ عَنْهُمْ).

In the *ḥadīth* of the Messenger of Allāh (ﷺ) is a warning from *bid'ah* (innovation), which is every newly innovated matter that a person introduces into the religion, which Allāh did not legislate and was not done by the Messenger of Allāh and his companions.

It also informs that every *bid'ah* (innovation) is misguidance. So the Muslim is not happy when division occurs among the Muslims, but when he or she encounters it they return to what Allāh and His Messenger instructed to do during those challenging times, which is holding fast to the *Qur'ān* and *Sunnah*. The Muslim also supplicates to Allāh that He keeps him or her firm upon the religion. The Prophet (صَلَّىٰ ٱللَّٰهُ عَلَيْهِ وَسَلَّمَ) used to supplicate with the follow supplication: "O Turner of the hearts, keep my heart firm upon Your religion."

Chapter Twenty-Five
A Warning Against Innovations in the Religion

O Muslim, the Prophet (ﷺ) warned from all innovations in the religion and informed that they are misguidance. He would say on Friday in the opening of the *Jumuʿah* sermon, "As to proceed: Beware of newly introduced matters, for every newly introduced matter is an innovation and every innovation is a misguidance and every misguidance is in the Hellfire."

This proves that all innovated matters within the religion are misguidance without any exception, due to the generality of the *ḥadīth*. There is no such thing as a good innovation (*bidʿah*) in Islām, as some people claim. Ibn ʿUmar (رَضِيَ ٱللَّٰهُ عَنْهُ) said:

> "Every innovation is misguidance, even if the people see it to be good."

That which is intended by newly introduced matters are those matters innovated and introduced in the religion. As for newly introduced matters in worldly affairs such as cars, planes, universities and the likes, then these are permissible and not religious innovations, although they may be called innovations linguistically.

Prophet Muḥammad (ﷺ) also said:

> "Whoever innovates into this affair of ours what is not from it, then it is rejected."

And in another wording:

> "Whoever does an action not in accordance with this affair of ours, then it is rejected."

This *ḥadīth* shows that whoever innovates something into the religion which has no origin, then it is rejected back upon the one who innovated it and it is not accepted. The second wording shows that it does not matter whether the one performing the innovated act originated it, or if they just acted upon it following behind someone else who originated and invented it; it still is rejected.

For this reason, it is incumbent upon you, O Muslim, to know what innovation is and how to recognize it, in order to stay away from it so your deeds may be accepted by Allāh and not rejected.

The scholars of Islām have defined innovation (*bidaʿ*) with numerous definitions, and here we will mention a few of them.

Ibn Taymiyyah (رَحِمَهُ ٱللَّهُ) said:

> "*Bidaʿ* (innovation) is everything that goes against the Book, *Sunnah* and the consensus of the *Salaf* of this *Ummah* from matters of belief and actions..."

Shaykh ʿUthaymīn said that innovation is:

> "Whatever is innovated in the religion opposite to what the Prophet (صَلَّى ٱللَّهُ عَلَيْهِ وَسَلَّمَ) and his companions were upon in matters of belief and action."

It has been defined as: "Whatever opposes the *Sunnah* from statement, actions or belief, even if it was based upon scholarly research and deduction."

Also, "Whatever is added to [an act of worship] from the customs of the disbelievers."

Also, "Extremism in worship."[1]

A person may ask why people innovate in the religion. There are many reasons behind this, from them:

One: Ignorance of rulings of the religion.

Two: Following of one's desires.

Three: Having fanaticism or over zealousness to a particular opinion (way) or person.

Four: Imitation of the disbelievers.[2]

---

[1] These last three were taken from "An Abridgement of the Rulings and Regulations Pertaining to the Funeral Rites" (p. 176) by *Shaykh* al-Albānī.

[2] See the book *'Aqīdah al-Tawḥīd* (p. 108) by *Shaykh* Ṣāliḥ al Fawzān.

The Dangers of Innovation

Innovation is very dangerous because when one introduces something new into the religion, it is as if they are saying that the religion is deficient and it is in need of additions. It is as if one is saying that the Prophet Muḥammad (صَلَّى ٱللَّهُ عَلَيْهِ وَسَلَّمَ) fell short in conveying what Allāh commanded him to convey. For this reason, Ibn Mājishūn (رَحِمَهُ ٱللَّهُ) said:

> "I heard Mālik say: 'Whoever innovates in Islām an innovation that they see to be good, then they (in reality) are claiming that Muḥammad failed to deliver the message (of Islām). This is because Allāh stated,
>
> "Today I have completed your religion for you."
>
> So whatever was not part of the religion that day will never be part of the religion.'"

So as you see, Allāh completed the religion for Muḥammad (صَلَّى ٱللَّهُ عَلَيْهِ وَسَلَّمَ). Whoever seeks to bring something new into it, they are saying by way of their actions - even if they do not say it out of their mouths - that Muḥammad (صَلَّى ٱللَّهُ عَلَيْهِ وَسَلَّمَ) did not properly convey the message, and there are things that they know of the religion that he did not, or that he did not convey to the people; and both of those possibilities are absurd and false.

So again, Allāh does not accept the actions of those who worship Him by way of innovations. Further, for any deed to be accepted by Allāh it must meet two conditions:

First: That it be done sincerely seeking the pleasure of Allāh.

Two: That it be done in the way that Prophet Muḥammad (صَلَّى ٱللَّٰهُ عَلَيْهِ وَسَلَّمَ) legislated it.

If one of these conditions is missing, Allāh does not accept that act worship. So if a person does an act of worship with sincerity for Allāh, but it is from among the innovations, Allāh will never accept it. This is because it is not in accordance with the *Sunnah* of Prophet Muḥammad (صَلَّى ٱللَّٰهُ عَلَيْهِ وَسَلَّمَ).

A clear example of this is an incident that occurred with one of the virtuous students of the companions by the name of Sa'īd Ibn Muṣayyib (رَحِمَهُ ٱللَّٰهُ) when he saw a man offering multiple (voluntary) prayers after the time of *fajr* entered, so he forbade him from doing so.

The man went on to say "Will Allāh punish me because of my prayer?" Sa'īd responded: "No, but He will punish you for opposing the *Sunnah.*[1]

So the base principle that the Muslim should know is that *all acts of worship are prohibited unless there is an evidence to prove its permissibility*. This is the origin. So one does not embark upon an act of worship unless there is a clear text that supports it. Additionally, one must restrict that act of worship to how the Prophet (صَلَّى ٱللَّٰهُ عَلَيْهِ وَسَلَّمَ) did it as far as the manner, place, time, number, and reason.

This is because an act of worship may be legislated in itself, but a person does it in other than the manner that the Prophet (صَلَّى ٱللَّٰهُ عَلَيْهِ وَسَلَّمَ) instructed, or in a place where Allāh and His messenger did not legislate, or by restricting it to a number that had not been legislated,

---

[1] See *Irwā' al-Ghalīl* (2/236).

or for a reason which Allāh and His Messenger did not make a reason.

For this reason, *al Ḥafidh* Ibn Rajab (رَحِمَهُ ٱللَّهُ) said:

> "Not every act [proven to be] a form of worship in a particular circumstance means that it is a form of worship [legislated] for every circumstance. Rather, as it pertains to this, that which is to be followed is what has come in the divine legislation, with its exact circumstances."[1]

Some Examples of Innovations in Statement and Action:

Making *dhikr* in a group.
Making *dhikr* with rocks or beads.
Making *du'ā'* to Allāh at the grave of a person considered to be righteous, believing it will more likely be answered.
Raising the hands to offer *du'ā'* after the obligatory prayers.
Placing the hand over the heart when giving *salāms* or after shaking hands.
Pronouncing the intention upon the tongue when doing an act of worship.
Making a habit to shake hands after the obligatory prayers, except if it's between two people who did not see each other before the prayer.
Kissing the *Musḥaf.*
Celebrating the birthday of the Prophet (صَلَّى ٱللَّهُ عَلَيْهِ وَسَلَّمَ).
Singing *Anāshīd* ("Islāmic songs").

---

[1] *Jāmi' al-'Ulūm wa al-Ḥikam* 1/178.

Some Examples of Innovations in ʿAqīdah (Belief):

Denying the Names and Attributes of Allāh that are established in the *Qur'ān* and *Sunnah*, asking how they occur, explaining them away from their apparent meanings, or resembling Allāh to His creation.

Belief that *Īmān* is only in the heart and is not accompanied by statement and action.

Belief that it is permissible to revolt and protest against the Muslim ruler, and spread his faults among the people due to some shortcomings he may have.

To believe that a Muslim becomes a disbeliever on the account of a major sin lesser than *Shirk* he or she has committed.

Speaking ill of and reviling the Companions of the Messenger of Allāh (ﷺ).

Belief that Allāh is everywhere. (The correct belief is that Allāh is above His Throne in a manner befitting His Majesty.)

Belief in pantheism (i.e. everything is Allāh and Allāh is everything).

Belief that Allāh becomes incarnate with some of His creation.

To deny anything from the divine decree of Allāh (*al-Qadr*).

- **Innovations is of two types:**

1. *Bidʿah Mukaffirah* that expels a person from the fold of Islam like the belief in Waḥdah al-Wujūd [that Allāh is everything and everything is Allāh].

2. *Bidʿah Mufassiqah* that does not expel a person from the fold of Islam, like group supplications.

The Position of the Muslim Against Those Who Innovate in the Religion and Spread Innovations:

The correct position as established by the texts of the *Qurʿān* and *Sunnah* prove is that the people of innovation are to be stayed away from and boycotted. This is because innovation is like a disease, and if you mix with those who practice and spread innovations, you can easily be affected by them. For this reason, Allāh and His Messenger warned from sitting with the people of innovation. This was understood by the companions and the Salaf as a whole, and they warned against innovations and its people.

Allāh says:

﴿ وَإِذَا رَأَيْتَ ٱلَّذِينَ يَخُوضُونَ فِىٓ ءَايَٰتِنَا فَأَعْرِضْ عَنْهُمْ حَتَّىٰ يَخُوضُوا۟ فِى
حَدِيثٍ غَيْرِهِۦ ۚ وَإِمَّا يُنسِيَنَّكَ ٱلشَّيْطَٰنُ فَلَا تَقْعُدْ بَعْدَ ٱلذِّكْرَىٰ مَعَ
ٱلْقَوْمِ ٱلظَّٰلِمِينَ ﴿٦٨﴾ ﴾

> **"And when you see those speaking who engage in false conversation about Our verses, stay away from them until they turn to another topic. And if shayṭān causes you to forget, then**

after remembrance, do not sit in the company of the people who are wrongdoers." [*al-An'ām* 6:68]

The scholar of *Tafsīr* Muḥammad Ibn Jarīr al-Ṭabarī (رَحِمَهُ ٱللَّهُ) said about this verse:

> "In this verse is a clear proof regarding the prohibition of sitting with the people of falsehood from every type, from the innovators and sinners when they engage in their false conversation."

The Prophet (صَلَّى ٱللَّهُ عَلَيْهِ وَسَلَّمَ) said to his wife 'Ā'ishah (رَضِيَ ٱللَّهُ عَنْهَا),

> "If you see those who follow the unclear and ambiguous verses (of the *Qur'ān*), then they are those who Allāh warned from, so beware of them."[1]

Ibn Abbās (رَضِيَ ٱللَّهُ عَنْهُمَا) said:

> "Do not sit with the people of desires, for sitting with them will surely bring sickness (i.e. doubts) to the hearts."

Ibn Mas'ūd (رَضِيَ ٱللَّهُ عَنْهُ) said,

> "Follow (i.e the *Sunnah*) and do not innovate, for indeed you have been given what is sufficient for you."

Fuḍayl Ibn 'Iyāḍ (رَحِمَهُ ٱللَّهُ) said:

[1] Refer to the Surah *Āl-'Imrān* 3:7.

> "Whoever sits with the person of innovation has not been given wisdom."

Imām al-Barbahārī (رَحِمَهُ ٱللَّهُ) said:

> "If you see a man sitting with a man from the people of desires, then warn him and inform him of (his condition), but if he sits with him after he knows about him, then stay away from him for he is a person of desires."

Ibn Qudāmah (رَحِمَهُ ٱللَّهُ) said:

> "And from the *Sunnah* is to boycott the people of innovation, and stay far away from them, and to leave off debating and arguing in the religion, and to leave looking in the books of the innovators and listening to their speech. Every newly introduced matter in the religion is an innovation."

Shaykh al-Islām Muḥammad Ibn ʿAbd al-Wahhāb (رَحِمَهُ ٱللَّهُ) said:

> "I see (the obligation) of boycotting the people of innovation and remaining distant from them until they repent. I judge them with what they make apparent, and I leave what they hold inside to Allāh. And I believe that every newly introduced matter in the religion is an innovation."

With all that which has preceded, it should be clear to you the harms and dangers of innovating in the religion and also the harms of sitting amongst the innovators and listening to them. So a person must closely guard those things that are precious to them, and there is nothing more precious than being upon pure and pristine guidance from Allāh. Therefore, one safeguards his or her religion from innovations because they taint and pollute the pure Islām and correct guidance. For this reason, we must always remain on guard from innovations and its people.

Chapter Twenty-Six
Must I follow a Madhhab[1]

A *madhhab* is positions and statements of a particular Imām related to matters of jurisprudence[2] that became famous and prominent among the Muslims. Some early scholars of Islām had students who dedicated themselves to spreading the statements of their teachers and then those statements and positions became widespread throughout the Islāmic world. There are four well known *madhhab*s that are attributed to four great Imāms of Islām. These four Imāms are:

Imām Abū Ḥanīfah (d.150H), and his *madhhab* is known as the *Ḥanafī Madhhab*.

Imām Mālik Ibn Anas (d.179H), and his *madhhab* is known as the *Mālikī Madhhab*.

Imām Muḥammad Ibn Idrīs al-Shāfiʿī (d.204H), and his *madhhab* is known as the *Shāfʿiʿī Madhhab*.

Imām Aḥmad Ibn Ḥanbal (d.241H), and his *madhhab* is known as the *Ḥanbalī Madhhab*.

There were other *madhhab*s of great scholars besides these four; however, they became extinct because their students did not

---

[1] A school of jurisprudence, such as the Ḥanafī, Mālikī, Shāfiʿī and Ḥanbalī schools.

[2] Such as statements regarding rulings of *fiqh* such as prayer, fasting, *ḥajj*, marriage, divorce and the likes.

continue to propagate their positions and statements, as was done with the aforementioned Imāms.
Attributing oneself to one of these *madhhab*s is permissible, either because one studied or is studying *fiqh* (jurisprudence) with a teacher who ascribes to one of these *madhhab*s, or because one grew up in a land where that *madhhab* is prominent. *However, none of these madhhabs are binding upon anyone from the Muslims to follow*, and we will mention some of the reasons that prove that.

There is no proof in the *Qur'ān*, or in the *Sunnah* of the Prophet Muḥammad (صَلَّىٱللَّهُعَلَيْهِوَسَلَّمَ) that makes it obligatory upon a person to follow one of these *madhhab*s or any other *madhhab*.

All of these Imāms came after the time of the Companions of Prophet Muḥammad (صَلَّىٱللَّهُعَلَيْهِوَسَلَّمَ) who were the best generation. Some of those Companions also had well known positions regarding jurisprudence, and if it were obligatory to follow anyone's position, then they would have been more deserving to be followed than anyone after them. No one from the scholars have ever stated that one must follow the *madhhab* of a particular companion, so all the more one does not have to follow a *madhhab* of someone who came years and years after them.

Allāh will not ask a person in the Hereafter why they did not follow a particular *madhhab*, rather Allāh will ask:

﴿ مَاذَآ أَجَبْتُمُ ٱلْمُرْسَلِينَ ﴾

"With what did you answer the Messengers?"
[*al-Qaṣaṣ* 28:65]

Meaning, did you deem them truthful and *follow them*, or did you deny them and oppose them?

So none of the statements of these Imāms came down as revelation from Allāh, and no one is infallible in what they state in the religion except Muḥammad (صَلَّى ٱللَّهُ عَلَيْهِ وَسَلَّمَ).

Some of the well-known students of some of these Imāms opposed the opinions of their teachers because they went against the explicit proof of the *Qur'ān* and *Sunnah*.

Many people have been afflicted with blind following of a *madhhab* to the point that if the position of their *madhhab* goes against a clear text of the *Qur'ān* or *ḥadīth*, they give precedence to their *madhhab* over the *Qur'ān* and *ḥadīth*. *This is haram (forbidden) by consensus of the scholars of Islām.*

We mentioned in an earlier chapter the statement of Allāh,

﴿ فَإِن تَنَٰزَعۡتُمۡ فِي شَيۡءٖ فَرُدُّوهُ إِلَى ٱللَّهِ وَٱلرَّسُولِ إِن كُنتُمۡ تُؤۡمِنُونَ بِٱللَّهِ وَٱلۡيَوۡمِ ٱلۡأٓخِرِۚ ذَٰلِكَ خَيۡرٞ وَأَحۡسَنُ تَأۡوِيلًا ﴾

> **"If you differ in anything then return it back to Allāh and His Messenger if you truly believe in Allāh and the Last Day. This is better for you and more suitable for final determination."** [*Al-Nisā'* 4:59]

So whatever the people differ in, it must be weighed in light of the *Qur'ān* and the *Sunnah* of the Messenger of Allāh (صَلَّى ٱللَّهُ عَلَيْهِ وَسَلَّمَ), and one must take what is established by the *Qur'ān* and *Sunnah*.

Therefore, if what Imām Aḥmad said is in accordance to the *Qur'ān* and *Sunnah* we take it, if not we reject it. If what Abū Ḥanīfah said is in accordance to the *Qur'ān* and *Sunnah* we take it, if not we reject it. This is true regarding all the scholars of Islām. This is because the *Qur'ān* and *Sunnah* are both revelation from Allāh. Therefore, one has no choice but to accept them, whereas the statements of men are prone to error, sometimes they are correct and sometimes they are incorrect.

For this very reason, each of these great Imāms instructed that if their statement goes against the statement of Allāh or His Messenger, to discard their statement and take the statement of Allāh and His Messenger (صَلَّى ٱللَّهُ عَلَيْهِ وَسَلَّمَ).

Imām Abū Ḥanīfah stated: "If a *ḥadīth* is proven to be correct, then it is my *madhhab*."

He also stated, "We are only human, we make a statement today, and retract from it tomorrow."

Imām Mālik said: "There is no one after the Prophet (صَلَّى ٱللَّهُ عَلَيْهِ وَسَلَّمَ) except that their statement can either be accepted or rejected."

Imām al-Shāfiʿī said: "If you see me to hold an opinion and its opposite has been authentically established upon the Prophet (صَلَّى ٱللَّهُ عَلَيْهِ وَسَلَّمَ), then know that I have lost my mind!"

Imām Aḥmad said: "Whoever rejects a *ḥadīth* of the Messenger of Allāh (صَلَّى ٱللَّهُ عَلَيْهِ وَسَلَّمَ), then they are upon the brink of destruction."

So, O Muslim, we have the utmost respect for the Imāms of Islām and their scholarly efforts and knowledge-based deductions, but by no means is the Muslim obligated to follow them if they contradict the statement of Allāh and His Messenger (صَلَّى ٱللَّهُ عَلَيْهِ وَسَلَّمَ). So beware of those who come to you claiming that you must pick a *madhhab* and staunchly adhere to it, and in particular today when many staunch *madhhab* followers hold innovated beliefs, which those Imāms that they claim to follow were free of.

Chapter Twenty-Seven
Who Are the Salaf?

In the Arabic language the word *Salaf* means what has preceded and came before you.

Allāh says in the *Qur'ān* after mentioning His punishment of the people of *Fir'awn*:

﴿فَجَعَلْنَٰهُمْ سَلَفًا وَمَثَلًا لِّلْءَاخِرِينَ ﴿٥٦﴾﴾

"And We made them a [Salaf] precedent and an example to later generations." [*Al-Zukhruf* 43:56]

So this is its meaning linguistically.

What is intended by the term *Salaf* in the aspect of the religion, then it is everyone who preceded you upon goodness, knowledge and correct belief, treading upon the Book of Allāh and the *Sunnah* of the Messenger of Allāh (صَلَّى ٱللَّٰهُ عَلَيْهِ وَسَلَّمَ). At the head of the *Salaf* are the three early generations of Muslims; the Companions of Prophet Muḥammad (صَلَّى ٱللَّٰهُ عَلَيْهِ وَسَلَّمَ), the generation after them and the generation after them.[1]

The scholar of Islām Muḥammad Amān al Jāmī said: "With us, the word *Salaf* is used to mean the Companions of the Messenger of Allāh (صَلَّى ٱللَّٰهُ عَلَيْهِ وَسَلَّمَ). They were those who were present during his time and they learned this religion from him directly and untainted

---

[1] Meaning the two generations after the Companions that adhered to the *Qur'ān* and *Sunnah* with the understanding of the Companions of the Messenger of Allah.

as it relates to its foundations and branches. Those who are included in this terminology are the *tābiʿīn* (i.e. generation after the companions) who inherited their knowledge before a great time elapsed (and people were taken by heedlessness). They are also those who are included in the Messenger's testimony of goodness for them and his praise for them that they are 'the best people'…"

He is alluding to the statement of Prophet Muḥammad (صَلَّى ٱللَّهُ عَلَيْهِ وَسَلَّمَ) when he said: "The best of people are my generation, then those who follow them and then those who follow them…" Reported by Bukhārī and Muslim.

So when the term *Salaf* is used, we are referring to the early generations of Muslims mentioned in the previous *ḥadīth*, who were the Companions of Prophet Muḥammad (صَلَّى ٱللَّهُ عَلَيْهِ وَسَلَّمَ), those who followed them and those who followed them. They were the best generations.

Furthermore, Allāh has praised those who follow the way of the Companions in exactness and precision.

He the Most High said:

﴿وَٱلسَّٰبِقُونَ ٱلۡأَوَّلُونَ مِنَ ٱلۡمُهَٰجِرِينَ وَٱلۡأَنصَارِ وَٱلَّذِينَ ٱتَّبَعُوهُم
بِإِحۡسَٰنٖ رَّضِيَ ٱللَّهُ عَنۡهُمۡ وَرَضُواْ عَنۡهُ وَأَعَدَّ لَهُمۡ جَنَّٰتٖ تَجۡرِي
تَحۡتَهَا ٱلۡأَنۡهَٰرُ خَٰلِدِينَ فِيهَآ أَبَدٗاۚ ذَٰلِكَ ٱلۡفَوۡزُ ٱلۡعَظِيمُ ١٠٠﴾

"The foremost to embrace Islām from the Muhājirūn and Anṣār, and those who follow them in exactness, Allāh is pleased with them and they with Him. And He has prepared for

them gardens beneath which rivers flow to abide therein forever. That is the supreme success." [*Al-Tawbah* 9:100]

The above verse proves that Allāh is pleased with those who follow the way of the Companions from the *Muhājirūn* and *Anṣār*, who were the *Salaf*.

This brings us to another point. Since Allāh is pleased with those who follow the *Salaf*, is it permissible to attribute oneself to their way? The answer is yes. One may attribute onself to these praiseworthy generations if it is done in truth. Meaning if one truly follows their way as it relates to belief, worship, and actions.

One may attribute oneself to them by saying "I am a *Salafī*." The letter i on the end of the word *Salaf* is equivalent to what is known in Arabic as *Yā Nisbah*, which shows affiliation and ascription. To make it clearer, if you were travelling abroad to an Arab country and you are from America, you would be known as *Amrīkī*, or the American, as an affiliation to your country. If a person was from Yemen for example, they are called *Yemenī*. So when you say you are *Salafī*, this is merely affiliating yourself to the way of the best generations, the *Salaf*.

One may say to you, there is nothing in the *Qur'ān* or *Sunnah* that commands one to call themselves *Salafī*, so one should stay away from it. The first response to this is that the words *Salaf* and *Salafī* are plentiful in the words of the early scholars of Islām. Second, we answer them with the tremendous statement of *Shaykh al-Islām* Ibn Taymiyyah, whose scholarship in the religion is well known by friend and foe.

He said:

"There is no blame on the one who professes the way of the *Salaf*, affiliates with it and ascribes to it; rather it is incumbent that it be accepted from him by agreement of the scholars, *for verily the way of the Salaf is nothing except the truth.*"[1]

[1] *Majmūʿ al-Fatāwā* (4/149).

Chapter Twenty-Eight
Be Careful From Whom You Take Your Religion

O Muslim, knowledge is not taken from just anyone. Not because a person says they have been Muslim for a significant amount of years, or because they were born into Islām, or because they are from a Muslim or Arab country, or because they wear a certain type of clothing or garment.

Knowledge likewise is not taken from the ignorant, nor from those who feign and pretend to be knowledgeable but have never sat down and learned from the scholars of Islām. Rather knowledge is taken from the firmly grounded scholars, known for their adherence to the Sunnah.

The great scholar Muḥammad Ibn Sīrīn used to say:

> "Verily, this knowledge is your religion, so examine carefully who you take your religion from." (Memorize)

Shaykh Ṣāliḥ al Fawzān said:

> "...Likewise, knowledge is not taken only from books and it is not taken from those who feign to have knowledge but have never sought understanding in the religion of Allāh. The most that can be said is that they read books or memorized something from the text and do not really comprehend its meaning and they have not understood it from the people of knowledge. This approach is harmful, because knowledge is only sought from the people of knowledge by taking directly

from them (in person) generation after generation, until Allāh inherits this earth and everyone upon it. So from the fundamentals of learning and from the essentials of learning is this matter; that it is taken from firmly grounded scholars who are known for knowledge that they sought from their scholars, and they then carry it on to their students and they pass it down amongst them, up until Allāh inherits the earth and everyone upon it. So this is from the fundamentals of seeking knowledge, that one travels to the scholars, and one seeks out the scholars in any place (they may be found) in order to take knowledge from them. This is the path which if one follows it, Allāh will make their path easy to *Jannah*."[1]

Shaykh Fawzān also said: "Those who ascribe themselves to giving *da'wah*, you must examine their affair (and find out) where did they study, and from whom did they take knowledge from, and where did they come from and what is their *'Aqīdah*. Allāh said:

﴿أَمْ لَمْ يَعْرِفُوا رَسُولَهُمْ فَهُمْ لَهُ مُنكِرُونَ ٦٩﴾

"Was it the fact that they did not know the Messenger as to reject him?" [*al-Mu'minūn* 23:69]

You also must look at their actions and their effects upon the people and what good did they bring about, and what rectification took place because of their actions. So it is a must to study their conditions before you are deceived by their outward appearance. This is a matter that is incumbent, especially in this time where the callers to tribulations have become abundant.

---

[1] A Glimpse at Some of the Etiquettes of the Seeker of Knowledge.

The Prophet (ﷺ) described the callers to tribulations that they will come from us and speak with our tongue. Also, when the Prophet (ﷺ) was asked about the tribulations he responded, "There will be *du'āt* (callers) at the gates of the Hellfire, whoever obeys them they will cast them into it."

Look how he called them *du'āt* (callers)! So it is upon us to pay attention to this and that we do not enlist for the purpose of *da'wah* just anybody, or everyone who says "I am calling to Allāh", or that such and such group is calling to Allāh. It is a must that we look at the reality of the matter, and that we look at the reality of groups and individuals…"[1]

What has preceded shows you that knowledge is taken from the scholars of Islām. It is upon you to travel to them, if you have the ability, and if not that you call them and ask them what concerns you from the matters of your religion. This no doubt stresses the importance of learning the Arabic language, as there are no scholars here in the West.

If you are unable to get to the scholars and sit at their feet, then at the very least try to sit with their students who have gone and sat with them and benefitted from them, those who have remained upon their way without changing or deviating, and whom have comprehended their speech, and are able to teach that to the people.

---

[1] *Al-Ajwibat al-Mufīdah* (p. 250).

Chapter Twenty Nine
Some Notable Scholars of Islām Past and Present

Here is a list of *some* of the firmly grounded scholars from the past to present:

Their deaths have been listed in the *hijrī* year. We are now in the year 1439 after the *Hijrah.*

ʿAbd al-Raḥmān Ibn ʿAmr al-Awzāʿī (d.157H)

Sufyān al-Thawrī (d.161H)
Ḥammād Ibn Salamah (d.167H)
Layth Ibn Saʿd (d.175H)
Mālik Ibn Anas (d.179H)
Ḥammād Ibn Zayd (d.179H)
Sufyān Ibn Uyaynah (d.197H)
Muḥammad Ibn Idrīs al-Shāfiʿī (d. 204H)

Abū ʿUbayd al-Qāsim Ibn Sallām (d.224H)
Aḥmad Ibn Ḥanbal (d.241H)

Muḥammad Ibn Ismāʿīl al-Bukhārī (d.256H)
Muslim Ibn Ḥajjāj al-Naysābūrī (d.261H)

ʿUthmān Ibn Saʿīd al-Dārimī (d.280H)

Abū Muḥammad al-Barbahārī (d.329H)
Abū Bakr al-Ājūrrī (d.360H)
Imām Ibn al-Baṭṭah al-ʿUkbarī (d.387H)

Abū 'Uthmān al-Ṣābūnī (d.449H)

Abū Muḥammad al-Baghawī (d. 516H)
Abd al-Ghanī al-Maqdisī (d. 600H)
Shaykh al-Islām Ibn Taymiyyah (d.728H)
Ibn al Qayyim al-Jawziyyah (d.751H)
Al-Ḥāfiẓ Ibn Kathīr (d.774H)
Al-Ḥāfiẓ Ibn Ḥajar al-'Asqalānī (d. 852H)
Shaykh al-Islām Muḥammad Ibn 'Abd al-Wahhāb (d.1206H)
Shaykh 'Abd al-Raḥmān Ibn Nāṣir al-Sa'dī (d.1376H)

Shaykh Ḥāfiẓ al-Ḥakamī (d.1377H)
Shaykh 'Abdullāh al-Qar'āwī (d.1389H)
Shaykh Muḥammad Amīn al-Shinqītī (d.1393H)
Shaykh Muḥammad al-Amān al-Jāmī (d.1416H)
Shaykh 'Umar al-Fallātah (d. 1418H)
Shaykh Ḥammād al-Anṣārī (d. 1418H)
Shaykh 'Abd al-'Azīz Ibn Bāz (d.1420H)
Shaykh Muḥammad Nāṣir al-Dīn al-Albānī (d.1420H)
Shaykh Muḥammad Ibn Ṣāliḥ al-'Uthaymīn (d.1421H)
Shaykh Muqbil Ibn Hādī al-Wādi'ī (d.1422H)
Shaykh Aḥmad al-Najmī (d.1429H)

Shaykh 'Abdullāh al-Ghudayyān (d. 1431H)
Shaykh Zayd al-Madkhalī (d.1435H)
Shaykh 'Abd al-Muḥsin al-'Abbād al-Badr (still living)

Shaykh Ṣāliḥ al-Fawzān (still living)
Shaykh Ṣāliḥ al-Luḥaydān (still living)
Shaykh Rabī' Ibn Hādī al-Madkhalī (still living)
Shaykh 'Ubayd Ibn 'Abdullāh al-Jābirī (still living)
Shaykh 'Alī Ibn Nāṣir al-Faqīhī (still living)

Chapter Thirty
Some Islāmic Mannerisms and Matters that Islām Has Forbidden

Islāmic Mannerisms:

Truthfulness
Being kind and dutiful to the parents
Honoring the elderly
Having mercy upon the young
Being kind to one's neighbors and not harming them
Spreading *Salām* to the Muslims
Smiling
Lowering the gaze (for men and women)
Not blocking the pathways and giving them their rights
Eating and drinking with the right hand
Taking and giving with the right hand
Saying *Bismillāh* before eating or drinking
Praising Allāh after eating or drinking
Saying *Alḥamdulillāh* after sneezing
Saying *YarḥamukAllāh* if a Muslim sneezes and says *Alḥamdulillāh*
Maintaining cleanliness
Visiting the sick
Feeding the poor
Giving charity
Following the funeral prayer and attending the burial of a Muslim
Maintaining Islāmic etiquettes when entering the Masjid, when entering and exiting your house, and when traveling.
Being just between your children
Consoling a Muslim who has a death in his family

Matters Islām has Forbidden:

Shirk

Killing an innocent soul without right

Indulging in interest and usury (*Ribā*)

Devouring the wealth of the orphan unjustly

Fornication (*Zinā*)

Homosexuality

Anal sex

Accusing chaste women (or men) or being fornicators of adulterers.

Disobeying the parents (unless they ask you to disobey Allāh)

Cutting off the ties of kinship

Bearing false testimony

Beating women

Oppressing people in regards to their blood, wealth, or honor. (i.e. shedding blood and theft)

Drinking intoxicants

Stinginess

Gambling

Backbiting Muslims (*Ghībah*)

Tail carrying between Muslims (*Namīmah*)

Stealing land or property

Celebrating birthdays or non-Muslim holidays[1]

Not paying those who worked or did a service for you, or paying people less than what they deserve

Taking the people of sin or innovations as companions

[1] There are only two celebrations in Islām which are *ʿĪd al-Fiṭr* which follows the fast of *Ramaḍān*, and *ʿĪd al-Aḍḥā* which occurs during the period of the obligatory *Ḥajj*.

Chapter Thirty One
A Glimpse at the Conduct of the Muslim Man and Mentioning Matters He Must Avoid

The Muslim man must be diligent in offering the five obligatory prayers in the *Masjid* if there is nothing that hinders him from getting to the *Masjid*.

He must be diligent upon attending the circles of knowledge in the known *Salafī Masjids*.

He should strive to keep a Muslim appearance and wear islāmic attire. This is by wearing the *thobe*, or the *izār* and the *kūfī*. The Muslim man should not allow his garment to drag below his ankles, as this is impermissible.

That goes for the *thawb*, *izār*, or pants/jeans. Wearing only pants/jeans is permissible, however they should be wide and hemmed above the ankles. The Prophet (صَلَّىٰ ٱللَّٰهُ عَلَيْهِ وَسَلَّمَ) said: "Whatever (garment) is below the ankles is in the Hellfire."

The Muslim man maintains cleanliness. He trims the mustache and allows the beard to grow without touching it by shaving or trimming it, as both are prohibited. He uses the *siwāk* (i.e. toothstick) before the prayer and when entering the house if possible. He also wears good smelling fragrance, especially when attending the *Jumuʿah* prayer.

The Muslim man should avoid hairstyles commonly worn by the disbelievers. The Prophet (صَلَّىٰ ٱللَّٰهُ عَلَيْهِ وَسَلَّمَ) forbade imitating the disbelievers in their outward ways and practices and said: "Whoever imitates a people is of them."

The Muslim man does not resemble the women by wearing bracelets, chains (including so-called Islāmic chains or bracelets), or earrings. The Prophet (صَلَّى ٱللَّهُ عَلَيْهِ وَسَلَّمَ) cursed the men who resemble the women and the women who resemble the men. However, it is permissible that the Muslim man wears a ring, so long as it is not made of gold.

The Muslim man should be diligent upon earning *ḥalāl* sources of income and staying away from all prohibited sources of income, whether that be from selling drugs, robbery, theft, or other than that. The Prophet Muḥammad (صَلَّى ٱللَّهُ عَلَيْهِ وَسَلَّمَ) said "Indeed Allāh is Good and He does not accept but what is good."

Once the Muslim man has a steady income he should rush to marry a Muslim woman with religion. Prophet Muḥammad (صَلَّى ٱللَّهُ عَلَيْهِ وَسَلَّمَ) said:

> "O youth, whoever from among you can afford maintaining a wife then let him marry, for verily it is better in keeping the gaze lowered and the private parts chaste."

He must go through her *walī* or *wakīl* when pursuing her or speaking with her. Any other ways may lead to what is forbidden and unpraiseworthy, such as fornication and/or an illegitimate child.

Once married, the marriage should be known and announced, as there are no secret marriages in Islām. *Shaykh* Ṣāliḥ al-Fawzān said: "It is legislated to announce the *nikāḥ* (marriage), thus the *nikāḥ* should not be secret, as to not resemble *zinā* (fornication); rather the *nikāḥ* should be announced… So these are the affairs that make the *nikāḥ* public; the presence of the *walī*, the (two upright) witnesses, beating the *duff*,[1] and having the *walīmah*;[2] all of this is from publicizing the *nikāḥ*. There is a clear difference between this and between philandering."

The Muslim man is a maintainer and protector of his wife and household. *He pays rent and bills, and provides food and clothing for his wife and children.* The Muslim male does not leave this duty upon his wife.

However, if the wife helps from her own accord and goodness, there is nothing wrong with that and she is rewarded. He makes sure his wife and kids are safe and does not allow any physical or religious harm to come to them, by the permission of Allāh.

The Muslim man should make his household a Muslim household. He should command his wife and children with the prayer and other obligatory acts and remain patient in doing so. He fills the house with the remembrance of Allāh and instills the Islāmic *'Aqīdah* within the members of his household.

He teaches them to have love for Allāh and His Prophet (صَلَّىٰٱللَّهُعَلَيْهِوَسَلَّمَ) and to follow his Sunnah. He also reminds them to have *taqwā* (i.e. fear) of Allāh, to abandon sins and disobeying Allāh, and to have a strong reliance and dependence upon Allāh alone, and not anyone from the creation.

The Muslim man should be just with his wife and allow for her time to learn the religion at classes in the *Masjid*. Prophet Muḥammad

---

[1] A small hand drum which the women are allowed to use on joyous occasions such as weddings.

[2] The feeding of the Muslims which is *Sunnah* to do three days after the marriage is consummated.

(صَلَّى ٱللَّٰهُ عَلَيْهِ وَسَلَّمَ) said: "Do not prevent the female slaves of Allāh from the houses of Allāh, and their homes are better for them."

The Muslim man is patient upon the shortcomings of his wife. Prophet Muḥammad (صَلَّى ٱللَّٰهُ عَلَيْهِ وَسَلَّمَ) informed that if you dislike a characteristic of the woman you will be pleased with another. He also informed that they were created having crookedness, as they were created from the rib of Ādam, and if you try to straighten her then you will break her, and breaking her means to divorce her.

So one remains patient with his wife and her shortcomings, so long as she is not doing what is clearly *ḥarām*, such as lewdness, uncovering, or leaving off the obligations such as the prayers.

If Allāh allows the Muslim man to have children, he should be diligent upon rearing them Islāmically, and he must give importance to them having an Islāmic education. He should also bring his sons to the *Masjid* when they reach an appropriate age and are no longer in constant need of the care of their mother.

He should also spend quality time with her and his children and not run the streets while his wife and children sit inside the house. In most cases this is a cause for an unhappy and unhealthy marriage. The Prophet (صَلَّى ٱللَّٰهُ عَلَيْهِ وَسَلَّمَ) said: "The best of you are the best towards his family, and I am the best among you as it relates to my family."

An example of those permissible places to take the family is museums, parks, walks, road trips, the beach, or simply to the *masjid* for classes or lectures. One should also make a goal to take his family to visit the land of the Muslims to perform *ḥajj* and/or *'umrah*.

The Muslim man should carry himself respectfully whilst outside of the house. He should speak to people politely, extend *salāms* to the

Muslims that he encounters, help those in need if he has the ability, and command the good and forbid the evil, so long as it is in the scope of what he is able to change, and it is done with knowledge and wisdom. He should not mock or laugh at the people, oppress or harm people, act in an obnoxious or foolish manner, or do anything that may cause people to look at Islām in a negative light.

The Muslim man should seek good and righteous companionship, such as with those striving to practice the religion and be upon uprightness and the *Sunnah*. He should stay away from frequenting places of disobedience that he may have before his Islām. He should distance himself away from evil companionship, and should not companion Muslims upon clear and open disobedience.
The Muslim man should stay away from conversing with women whom it is permissible for him to marry, except when necessary.

The Muslim man does not date or have illicit relations with women on the side, whether they be Muslim women or non-Muslim women. Likewise, he does not chat with or follow women on social media sites such as Facebook, Instagram and Twitter, as this is a path to *ḥarām* relationships, and *zinā* (fornication or adultery).

Chapter Thirty-Two
The Proper Dress Code of the Muslim Woman

Dear Muslim sister, Allāh has given you a lofty status in Islām and has honored you by legislating the *ḥijāb*. The history of the Muslims has shown that the woman clinging steadfast to what Allāh legislated, as well as the manners and etiquettes of Islām, is the best and most successful way that they bring benefit and rectification to the Muslim community.

History has also shown that her wearing the *ḥijāb* and *jilbāb* has always been a reason for her preservation and protection. Much of the corruption witnessed today is a result of immodest behavior and improper covering.

The adversaries of Islām, the hypocrites and their likes, are enraged due to this lofty status, honor, and nobility Islām has given you. They know they cannot come to you and tell you to commit *Shirk* (associate partners with Allāh in worship) or fall into disbelief; however, they want you to be an easy prey and a target for the wolves from mankind who are plagued with sick hearts.

They make the affairs of free mixing with men, dressing in a lustful manner, and adopting the customs and practices of the disbelievers fair seeming in the name of freedom, women's rights, liberalism, and other slogans. The end result of this is the crumbling of the Muslim community at its very foundation: the Muslim woman.

We all are eye witnesses to the devastation within the communities because of the women free mixing with men and their open display of their beauty. This has resulted in countless illegitimate children without fathers, broken households, struggling mothers, many diseases, and sometimes even murder. For this reason, the Muslim woman must be farsighted and ponder how these calls to "freedom" or uncovering directed at her are in reality aimed to destroy Islām from within.

In order to protect your honor, nobility, and shyness, Allāh legislated for you the wearing of the *Jilbāb* in the presence of all men who are not your husband or *maḥram* (i.e. unmarriageable male relatives such as the father, grandfather, uncle, brother, son, stepson, and nephew).

Allāh says:

﴿يَٰٓأَيُّهَا ٱلنَّبِيُّ قُل لِّأَزْوَٰجِكَ وَبَنَاتِكَ وَنِسَآءِ ٱلْمُؤْمِنِينَ يُدْنِينَ عَلَيْهِنَّ مِن
جَلَٰبِيبِهِنَّ ذَٰلِكَ أَدْنَىٰٓ أَن يُعْرَفْنَ فَلَا يُؤْذَيْنَ﴾

> **"O Prophet! Tell your wives, daughters and believing women to draw their Jilbābs all over their bodies. This is better for them to be known as believing women as to not be harmed."** [*Al-Aḥzāb*: 33:59]

The *Jilbāb* is the large, wide cloak that covers the woman's entire body. Allāh commanded His Prophet to tell his wives, daughters and the believing woman to draw the *Jilbāb* over their body. This command from Allāh shows that this matter is obligatory for all believing Muslim women, and not merely optional.

Conditions of the *Jilbāb*:

1. That the *Jilbāb* covers the whole entire body

2. That the *Jilbāb* itself not be adorned or eye-catching.
3. That the *Jilbāb* be thick and not transparent.
4. That the *Jilbāb* be wide and not tight whereas the shape of the woman's body can be seen.
5. That the *Jilbāb* is not perfumed or scented.
6. That the *Jilbāb* does not resemble the clothing of the men.
7. That the *Jilbāb* does not resemble the clothing of the disbelieving women.

A Warning from al-Tabarruj (i.e. the Muslim woman improperly displaying her beauty):

Allāh, the Exalted, warns the Muslim women from *al-Tabarruj* in many places in the *Qur'ān*.

He said:

﴿ وَقَرْنَ فِي بُيُوتِكُنَّ وَلَا تَبَرَّجْنَ تَبَرُّجَ ٱلْجَٰهِلِيَّةِ ٱلْأُولَىٰ ۖ وَأَقِمْنَ
ٱلصَّلَوٰةَ وَءَاتِينَ ٱلزَّكَوٰةَ وَأَطِعْنَ ٱللَّهَ وَرَسُولَهُۥٓ ﴾

"And stay in your houses, and do not display yourselves like that of the times of ignorance, and perform al-Ṣalāt, and give Zakāt and obey Allāh and His Messenger." [*al-Ahzāb* 33:33]

And He, the Most High said:

﴿ وَقُل لِّلْمُؤْمِنَٰتِ يَغْضُضْنَ مِنْ أَبْصَٰرِهِنَّ وَيَحْفَظْنَ فُرُوجَهُنَّ وَلَا
يُبْدِينَ زِينَتَهُنَّ إِلَّا مَا ظَهَرَ مِنْهَا ۖ وَلْيَضْرِبْنَ بِخُمُرِهِنَّ عَلَىٰ جُيُوبِهِنَّ ۖ
وَلَا يُبْدِينَ زِينَتَهُنَّ إِلَّا لِبُعُولَتِهِنَّ أَوْ ءَابَآئِهِنَّ أَوْ ءَابَآءِ
بُعُولَتِهِنَّ أَوْ أَبْنَآئِهِنَّ أَوْ أَبْنَآءِ بُعُولَتِهِنَّ أَوْ إِخْوَٰنِهِنَّ أَوْ
بَنِىٓ إِخْوَٰنِهِنَّ أَوْ بَنِىٓ أَخَوَٰتِهِنَّ أَوْ نِسَآئِهِنَّ أَوْ مَا مَلَكَتْ أَيْمَٰنُهُنَّ
أَوِ ٱلتَّٰبِعِينَ غَيْرِ أُو۟لِى ٱلْإِرْبَةِ مِنَ ٱلرِّجَالِ أَوِ ٱلطِّفْلِ ٱلَّذِينَ لَمْ
يَظْهَرُوا۟ عَلَىٰ عَوْرَٰتِ ٱلنِّسَآءِ ۖ وَلَا يَضْرِبْنَ بِأَرْجُلِهِنَّ لِيُعْلَمَ مَا يُخْفِينَ

مِن زِينَتِهِنَّۚ وَتُوبُوٓاْ إِلَى ٱللَّهِ جَمِيعًا أَيُّهَ ٱلۡمُؤۡمِنُونَ لَعَلَّكُمۡ
تُفۡلِحُونَ ٣١

"Tell the believing men to lower their gaze (from looking at forbidden things), and protect their private parts (from illegal sexual acts, etc.). That is purer for them. Verily, Allāh is All-Aware of what they do. And tell the believing women to lower their gaze (from looking at forbidden things), and protect their private parts (from illegal sexual acts, etc.) and not to show off their adornment except only that which is apparent, (such as the hands and outer garment) and to draw their veils all over Juyūbihinna (i.e. their bodies, faces, necks and bosoms, etc.) and not to reveal their adornment except to their husbands, their fathers, their husband's fathers, their sons, their husband's sons, their brothers or their brother's sons, or their sister's sons, or their (Muslim) women (i.e. their sisters in Islām), or the (female) slaves whom their right hands possess, or old male servants who lack vigor, or small children who have no sense of the shame of sex. And let them not stamp their feet so as to reveal what they hide of their adornment. And all of you beg Allāh to forgive you all, O believers, that you may be successful." [*al-Nūr* 24:31]

The Prophet Muḥammad (ﷺ) said in an authentic *ḥadīth*:

> "There are two types who will be in the Hellfire that I have yet to see: a people who have whips resembling the tails of cows using them to beat the people, *and women who are clothed, yet naked.* They are leaning (from the way of truth) causing others to lean (away from the truth); their heads will be (shaped) like leaning camel humps. They will not enter Paradise nor will they smell its fragrance; its fragrance can be smelled from such and such a distance."

These are just some of the many texts of the *Qur'ān* and *Sunnah* that prohibit the Muslim woman from improperly displaying her beauty.

Some Manifestations of al-Tabbaruj:

- Not wearing the *khimār* (head-covering)
- Not wearing the *jilbāb* (but wearing jeans, scrubs, skirts, or shorts instead)
- Wearing the *khimār*, but with the hair, ears, or neck exposed, or with the earrings showing
-Wearing a tight *jilbāb* that shows the curves of the body
-Wearing a belt around the waist over the *jilbāb*, because this displays the curves of the body
-Wearing *jilbāb*s with decoration on them
-Wearing a *jilbāb* that is transparent (i.e. see through)
-Wearing the *jilbāb* on the shoulders, as opposed to over the head, covering the Khimar and draping down to the feet
-Wearing high heels (outside of the home)
-Wearing sandals without socks (outside of the home)
-Exiting the home wearing perfume, scents, or fragrances
-Exiting the home wearing makeup, mascara, kohl on the eyes, lipstick, or glossy lip balm

Some Manifestations that Contradict the Muslim Woman's Modesty:

- Dating men, whether they be Muslim or Non-Muslim
- Talking loudly and joking in front of, or near men who are non-*maḥram*
-Unnecessarily holding conversations with men who are non-*maḥram*
-Flirting, joking, smiling, laughing, or talking in soft and alluring tones with non-*maḥram* men
-Conversing with non- *maḥram* men who inquire about marriage, without the presence of your *walī*, or *wakīl*

-Posting pictures and selfies online or on social media
-Mixing freely with men
-Going out to clubs, parties, and after-hours establishments
-Travelling without a *maḥram*

In closing dear Sister, you are a Queen beneath your *ḥijāb*, so feel honored and be proud of your Religion, and the status Allāh has given you. Preserve your dignity and nobility, and implement what He commanded you with from proper covering, shyness, and modesty. There are many temptations of worldly pleasure and desire, especially here in the West, but the approaching of the hour is only a twinkling of the eye, or even nearer. If you implement what Allāh commanded you with and are patient, you have a wondrous and everlasting reward awaiting you in the Hereafter with your Lord, if Allāh wills.

May Allāh bless you and keep you firm upon the *Qur'ān* and *Sunnah*.

Chapter Thirty-Three
Patience and Its Three Types[1]

Dear Muslim, patience has a tremendous status in the religion, and for this reason Allāh has commanded the believers with it. Patience has been mentioned in the *Qur'ān* around ninety times, as stated by Imām Aḥmad. Allāh mentioned that the patient ones will be given their reward without limit, and He mentioned that He is with those who are patient; meaning that He is with them with His aid and help.

It also comes in the *ḥadīth* of the Prophet (صَلَّى ٱللَّٰهُ عَلَيْهِ وَسَلَّمَ):

"And patience is an illumination…"

Also he (صَلَّى ٱللَّٰهُ عَلَيْهِ وَسَلَّمَ) said:

> "No one has been given anything better and vaster than patience."

The scholars have defined patience as:

Withholding the soul from becoming upset and agitated, withholding the tongue from complaining and bemoaning, and withholding the limbs from smacking the faces and ripping the pockets.[2]

---

[1] Taken from the words of *Shaykh* al-'Uthaymīn and *Shaykh* Fawzān with slight alteration.

[2] These are practices done by some people when calamity strikes, and it is not limited to these actions, rather any action done at times of calamities that are not legislated in Islām, such as pouring out liquor, listening to music, getting high etc.

As for patience itself, the scholars have mentioned that it is of three types:

The First: Patience in performing the acts of obedience.

An example of this is having patience in performing the obligatory prayers. The time for prayer may enter but one's soul favors laziness at that time, or sleep, or conversing with friends. However, this person forces himself to get up and perform the prayer. This is patience upon the obedience of Allāh.

The Second: Patience in staying away from the acts of disobedience.

An example of this is that a person may want to commit fornication- may Allāh protect us from that- but he or she practices patience and prevents their soul from doing so for Allāh's sake. This is patience in staying away from the acts of disobedience.

The Third: Patience upon the painstaking decrees of Allāh, the Most High.

An example of this is that Allāh may decree for a person a loss of wealth, loss of a loved one, health problems or the likes. Here, it is incumbent upon the believer to remain patient with what Allāh decreed.

Allāh says:

﴿ وَلَنَبْلُوَنَّكُم بِشَيْءٍ مِّنَ الْخَوْفِ وَالْجُوعِ وَنَقْصٍ مِّنَ الْأَمْوَالِ
وَالْأَنفُسِ وَالثَّمَرَاتِ ۗ وَبَشِّرِ الصَّابِرِينَ ﴿١٥٥﴾ الَّذِينَ إِذَا أَصَابَتْهُم
مُّصِيبَةٌ قَالُوا إِنَّا لِلَّهِ وَإِنَّا إِلَيْهِ رَاجِعُونَ ﴿١٥٦﴾ أُولَٰئِكَ عَلَيْهِمْ صَلَوَاتٌ مِّن
رَّبِّهِمْ وَرَحْمَةٌ ۖ وَأُولَٰئِكَ هُمُ الْمُهْتَدُونَ ﴿١٥٧﴾ ﴾

"And certainly, We shall test you with something of fear, hunger, loss of wealth, lives and provisions, but give glad tidings to the patient ones. Who, when afflicted with calamity, say: 'Truly to Allāh we belong and truly, to Him we shall return.' They are those on whom are blessings from their Lord and who will receive His Mercy, and it is they who are the rightly guided." [*Al-Baqarah* 2:155-157]

Allāh also says:

﴿ مَا أَصَابَ مِن مُّصِيبَةٍ إِلَّا بِإِذْنِ اللَّهِ ۗ وَمَن يُؤْمِن بِاللَّهِ يَهْدِ قَلْبَهُ ۚ ﴾

"No calamity befalls but with the permission of Allāh, and whosoever believes in Allāh, He guides his heart." [*Al-Taghābun* 64:11]

ʿAlqamah from the *salaf* said about this verse:

> "It is the person who is afflicted with a calamity and knows that it has been decreed by Allāh, so he is pleased and submits."

This shows that patience is from *Īmān*, and that the believer is in need of patience in all of his affairs. He or she is in need of patience as it relates to the commands and prohibitions of Allāh, likewise as it relates to the calamities and misfortunes that may befall them. They realize that they were decreed by Allāh and they submit and are pleased. Similarly, they withhold themselves from what may occur by way of the tongue and limbs from complaining and doing impetuous actions. This also shows that patience has a direct relation to *ʿAqīdah*, and that is the belief in the divine decree (*qadar*), one of the six pillars of *Īmān*.

So from the fruits of belief in the divine decree is remaining patient upon calamities. So whoever does not remain patient upon calamities, this shows that this great pillar is missing or it has weakness within a person. The result of this is that a person will be imprudent and reckless when confronting calamities.

Allāh decrees calamities upon His servants due to wisdoms that only He knows. It has been reported in the authentic hadith that the Messenger of Allāh said:

> "If Allāh wants good for His servant, He hastens for him his punishment in this life. If He wants evil for a servant, He does not seize him because of his sins, until he comes forth with all of that on the Day of Resurrection."

Ibn Taymiyyah said:

> "Calamities are a favor from Allāh; they invite to having patience and also expiate the sins of a servant and he is rewarded for them. They also cause one to sincerely return to Allāh and have humility before Him, turning away from the creation (for help). And other benefits besides these..."

The Prophet (صَلَّى ٱللَّهُ عَلَيْهِ وَسَلَّمَ) said:

> "Indeed, the greatness of reward comes with the greatness of the trial, and if Allāh loves a people, He puts them through trials. Whoever is pleased will receive pleasure (from Allāh) and whoever is displeased will receive displeasure (from Allāh)."

Pleasure here means that the servant submits his affair to Allāh, has good thoughts of Him and eagerly awaits His reward. The meaning of displeasure is that one has hatred of a matter and is not pleased. So what is intended is that whoever is displeased with what Allāh decreed for him, then upon him will be displeasure from Allāh.

Also, the Prophet (صَلَّى ٱللَّهُ عَلَيْهِ وَسَلَّمَ) said:

> "How amazing is the affair of the believer! Indeed, all of his affair is good, and this is for none other than the believer. If good befalls him, he is thankful and that is better for him. And if a calamity befalls him, he is patient and that is better for him."

Chapter Thirty-Four
Repentance and Its Conditions[1]

Dear Muslim, Allāh has made obligatory that one turns to Him in repentance for every sin that they commit. It is incumbent upon the one who falls short and commits a sin to rush to repent without delay.

Allāh says:

﴿ وَتُوبُوٓا۟ إِلَى ٱللَّهِ جَمِيعًا أَيُّهَ ٱلْمُؤْمِنُونَ لَعَلَّكُمْ تُفْلِحُونَ ﴾

"And all of you turn to Allāh in repentance, O believers, that you may be successful." [*Al-Nūr* 24:31]

The greatest type of repentance is to repent from *shirk* and *kufr* (disbelief) to *Īmān*. Allāh the Most High said:

﴿ قُل لِّلَّذِينَ كَفَرُوٓا۟ إِن يَنتَهُوا۟ يُغْفَرْ لَهُم مَّا قَدْ سَلَفَ وَإِن
يَعُودُوا۟ فَقَدْ مَضَتْ سُنَّتُ ٱلْأَوَّلِينَ ﴿٣٨﴾ ﴾

"Say to those who have disbelieved, if they cease (from disbelief) their past will be forgiven. But if they return (thereto), then the examples of those (punished) before them have already preceded (as a warning)." [*Al-Anfāl* 8:38]

---

[1] Most of this is taken from the explanation of *Riyāḍ al-Ṣāliḥīn* by *Shaykh* al-ʿUthaymīn.

What follows that is the obligation to repent from major sins, such as killing unjustly, fornication, and consuming intoxicants, and what follows that is the obligation to repent from the minor sins.

Further, Allāh the Most High loves when His servants turn to Him in repentance. Allāh mentions in the *Qur'ān*:

﴿إِنَّ ٱللَّهَ يُحِبُّ ٱلتَّوَّٰبِينَ وَيُحِبُّ ٱلْمُتَطَهِّرِينَ﴾

> **"Truly Allāh loves those who turn to Him in repentance and loves those who purify themselves."** [*al-Baqarah* 2:222]

And the Prophet (صَلَّىٰ ٱللَّهُ عَلَيْهِ وَعَلَىٰ آلِهِ وَسَلَّمَ) said:

> "Indeed, Allāh is happier at the repentance of His servant when he repents than one of you who was upon his riding mount in a desolate land, which ran away from him and upon it was his food and drink. Up until the point he lost all hope of finding it. So he goes and takes shade under a tree [awaiting death], having given up all hope of finding his riding mount. So as he was in this state, he looks up and finds his mount standing above him, and snatches it by its reins…"

Also, he (صَلَّىٰ ٱللَّهُ عَلَيْهِ وَعَلَىٰ آلِهِ وَسَلَّمَ) said:

> "Verily, Allāh extends His Hand by night so the one who did badly during the day can repent, and He extends His Hand by day, so the one who did badly during the night can repent, up until the sun rises from its West."

Also know, may Allāh have mercy upon you, that repentance has four conditions.[1]

The First: That one must stop and cease committing that sin. And if the sin occurred by leaving off an obligation, such as giving the obligatory zakat, stopping the sin occurs by paying the *zakāt.*

The Second: To have regret and remorse. This is because when a person feels remorse due to committing a sin, this shows that he or she is sincere in their repentance.

The Third: To have strong determination not to ever return back to that sin.

These three conditions are binding if the sin is between a servant and his Lord. However, if the sin committed relates to the right of a human being, then there is a fourth condition along with the three above, which is to return the right back to whom it is due.

So for example, if one stole money from a person they must return it. If one slandered or backbit a Muslim, they must go and seek their pardon and ask to be absolved from that[2], and so on and so forth.

One should know that so long as he or she has life in their soul, they can repent from their sins. Even if one repented from a sin and returned back to it, they must return and repent to Allāh again, even if this happens several times. One should not let the thought come

---

[1] Some of the scholars mention five conditions

[2] The scholars mention that if one thinks that going to the person and informing them of the backbiting or slander will result in a greater harm, then they should not inform them but they should suffice by mentioning that person with good in those sittings where they spoke ill of him or her. Also they offer *du'ā'* for that person, by saying for example "O Allāh, forgive so and so."

to them which is: “You keep returning to such and such sin, Allāh will never forgive you.” This is an evil thought from *shayṭān*, and one must seek refuge with Allāh from it.

There comes in an authentic *ḥadīth* of a man who killed ninety nine men and sought repentance. When he went and asked a man who was a devout worshipper but was ignorant, the man told him he could not repent, so he killed him too. Then he inquired from a man who possessed knowledge. The man’s response was:

> “Who is it that can come between you and repentance? However, you are in an evil land. Depart from this land, and go to a land where they worship Allāh…”

This man took the advice of the learned man and ended up being from the people of Paradise.

So, O Muslim, Allāh is swift and severe in punishment, but He also is the Oft-Forgiving, the One who frequently accepts the repentance of His servants (*al-Tawwāb*), and He is the Most Merciful.

If you turn to Allāh with sincere repentance with its conditions, then Allāh accepts the repentance of those who repent, no matter how great the sin is.

Chapter Thirty-Five
What Does Islām Say About *Jihād* and Extremism?[1]

O Muslim. You have most likely heard of and seen in the media barbaric acts of terrorism, killings, bombings and the likes that many times are attributed to Islām and the Muslims. In this chapter we would like to examine what Islām says about *Jihād*, bombings, terrorism, and groups such as ISIS and *al-Qāʿidah.*

Jihād in Islām is of different types. From that is *Jihād* against one's souls which is to struggle against one's lusts and desires and to fight them in order to obey Allāh and stay away from disobeying Him. Similarly, from its types is *Jihād* with the pen, and this is for those with knowledge who defend Islām by writing books in order to refute those who attach to this noble religion lies and fabrications, whether that be from the people of innovation and misguidance within Islām, or those outside of Islām such as the Jews, Christians, or other than them.

There is also *Jihād* upon the battlefield in a conventional war. This has guidelines and important principles, and it is not for just anyone to declare *Jihād*. War in Islām is declared by leaders and governments, not individual citizens, insurgents or preachers who call to *Jihād* during Friday sermons or through social media. These independent declarations of *Jihād* and warfare carry no legitimacy in Islām. Furthermore, in the legislated *Jihād*, it is not permissible to kill

[1] Most of this has been taken from the pamphlet "Combatting 21st Century Violent Extremist Terrorism" compiled by Salafi Publications out of Birmingham, UK. Return to their website for the full pamphlet and other beneficial material.

non-combatants, such as women, children, monks, teachers, doctors, and the elderly. The Jihādist claim that all non-Muslims are legitimate targets runs contrary to Islāmic teachings.

The appearance of the ideology of ISIS, *al-Qā'idah* and those like them is actually not a new phenomenon. Muslim governments over centuries have encountered these types of rebellious movements known in Islāmic terminology as the *Khawārij* or Kharijites. These individuals are none other than blood thirsty criminals who desire to spread corruption to attain their political goals in the name of Islām. You find the vast majority of these terrorists are ignorant of the basic teachings of Islām, such as *Tawḥīd*, and the rulings on purification and prayer.

One should not be deceived by the outward display of piety among some of these terrorists, such as prayer, fasting, and their claim to have love for Islām. Prophet Muḥammad (صَلَّى ٱللَّهُ عَلَيْهِ وَسَلَّمَ) said regarding the *Khawārij*:

"One of you will belittle your prayer next to their prayer, and your fast next to their fast, and your recitation next to their recitation; but they will exit Islām faster than an arrow goes through the hunted animal."

The *Salafī* scholar Imām *al-Ājūrrī* said regarding them,

> "Neither the scholars of old, nor of these times ever differed about the Kharijites. *They regarded them as an evil people who were disobedient to Allāh and His Messenger* even though they prayed, fasted and exerted themselves in worship. And all of this was of no benefit to them."

So as you see, so long as they are upon this evil path, their outward display of worship and piety will be of no benefit. Rather they are considered to be included among the deviant misguided sects of the Muslims who are under the threat of being punished in the Hellfire. The Prophet Muḥammad (صَلَّىٰ ٱللَّهُ عَلَيْهِ وَسَلَّمَ) referred to the *Khawārij* as "Dogs of the Hellfire."

So if a Muslim encounters a person who has the ideology of the *Khawārij*, he must not argue or debate with him, nor does he sit with him or befriend him. He flees from him as he would flee from a lion.

If a Muslim knows that one of these individuals is plotting to hurt or kill someone, whether they be Muslim or non-Muslim, it is incumbent to inform the authorities. *This is not considered snitching*. This is considered commanding the good and forbidding the evil, a duty which Allāh and His Messenger made obligatory upon the Muslims according to each person's ability.

Chapter Thirty-Six
Some Recommended Books to Read

The Noble Qur'ān - Translation of Muḥammad Muḥsin Khan and Hilali.

Summarized Sahih Bukhari - Translation Muḥammad Muḥsin Khan

Summarized Sahih Muslim (2 Volumes) - Printed by Darrusalam

The Three Fundamental Principles Study Guide - Salafi Publications

Explanation of the Three Fundamental Principles - *Shaykh* Muḥammad Ibn Ṣāliḥ al-'Uthaymīn - Translation Dawud Burbank – al-Hidayah Publications

A Gift to the Intellects in Explaining the Three Fundamental Principles - *Shaykh* 'Ubayd al-Jābirī

Al-'Aqīdah al-Wasitiyyah – *Shaykh* al-Islām Ibn Taymiyyah - Dar as *Sunnah* Publishers

Foundations of the *Sunnah* by Imām Aḥmad - Salafi Publications

The Creed of the *Salaf* and the People of *Hadīth* by Abū 'Uthmān al-Ṣābūnī

The Creed by Abu Muḥammad al-Barbaharee - Translated by Dawud Burbank

Fundamental Beliefs of a Muslim - *Shaykh* Ṣāliḥ al-Fawzān - Hikmah Publications

Kitab al-Tawḥīd - Explained by *Shaykh* Ṣāliḥ al-Fawzān

Explanation of Important Lessons - *Shaykh* 'Abdur-Razzaq al-'Abbād - Authentic Statements Publications

A Glimpse at the Impeccable Characteristics of the Noble Prophet - *Shaykh* 'Abdul-Muḥsin al-'Abbad al-Badr - Hikmah Publications

The Prophet and His Ten Companions Who Were Promised Paradise - Ibn Qudāmah al-Maqdisī - Authentic Statements Publications

The Prophet's Prayer Described- *Shaykh* Muḥammad Nāṣir al-Dīn al-Albānī- Dar us Sunnah Publishers

The Abridged Prophet's Prayer Described - *Shaykh* al-Albānī - Salafi Publications

Description of the Regular *Sunnah* Prayers - *Shaykh* Muḥammad Bāzmūl

Methodology of the Prophets in calling to Allāh - *Shaykh* Rabīʿ al-Madkhalī - Hidayah Publications

Mountains of Knowledge - Salafi Publications

Things that Nullify one's Islām - Explained by *Shaykh* Ṣāliḥ al-Fawzān - TROID Publications

Al-Wājibāt - The Obligatory Matters That Must Be Known by Every Muslim Male and Female - explained by *Shaykh* Aḥmad al-Najmī - Hikmah Publications

Reasons for Deviation from the Truth - *Shaykh* Rabīʿ al-Madkhalī - Salafi Publications

The Precise Verdicts Regarding Deviant Methodologies - *Shaykh* Aḥmad al-Najmī - Sunnah Publishing

The Autobiography of Muqbil Ibn Hādee al Wādiʿī - Compiled by Abū al-Ḥasan Mālik - Al-Rahmaniyyah Press

The Misguidance of the Ḥabashī Sect - by the Permanent Committee of Scholars

Abridged Rulings and Regulations on the Funeral Prayer in Islām - *Shaykh* al-Albānī - Hikmah Publications

The Keys to Happiness - Ibn al-Qayyim - Hikmah Publications

The Noble Revered Prophet Muḥammad - Abū Iyad Amjad Rafiq

The Wahhabi Myth - Haneef Oliver - TROID Publications

Summarized Jurisprudence - *Shaykh* Ṣāliḥ al-Fawzān (2 vol. Hardback)

An Explanation of the Four Principles - *Shaykh* Ṣāliḥ al-Fawzān - Salafi Publications

Explanation to the Beautiful and Perfect Names of Allāh - *Shaykh* Saʿdī - Dar as-Sunnah Publishers

Facilitation by Allāh in Explanations the Conditions of La ilaha illa Allāh - *Shaykh* 'Ubayd al-Jābirī

Prophetic Ahadith in Condemnation of Racism - *Shaykh* Abdus Salam ibn Burjiss - Sunnah Publishing

Fundamentals of the *Salafee* Methodology - *Shaykh* Muḥammad Nāṣir al-Dīn al-Albānī - TROID Publications

The Creed of the Four Imaams - Dr. Muḥammad al-Khumayyis - TROID Publications

Important Lessons for Ramaḍān - *Shaykh* 'Abdur-Razzaq al-'Abbād - Hikmah Publications

A Collection of Treatises for *Ahlus-Sunnah* on How to Deal With the People of Innovation- *Shaykh* 'Ubayd al-Jābirī - Miraath Publications

A Woman's Guide to Raising a Family - *Shaykh* Ṣāliḥ al-Fawzān - Hikmah Publications

Explanation of the Supplications for the Sick and Afflicted - *Shaykh* 'Abdur-Razzāq al-'Abbād - Hikmah Publications

The Rights of the Parents in Light of the *Qur'ān* and Sunnah - *Shaykh* Muḥammad Bāzmūl - Sunnah Publishing

The Status of the Messenger and his Rights - *Shaykh* Rabī' al-Madkhalī

A Piece of Advice and Admonition for the Women - *Shaykh* 'Abdur-Razzāq al-'Abbād - Hikmah Publications

Jesus in Islām, Christianity, and the Jewish Talmud - Amjad Rafiq

Explanation of the 'Aqīdah of the Imām, the Reformer, Muḥammad Ibn 'Abdul-Wahhab - *Shaykh* Ṣāliḥ al-Fawzān - Sunnah Publishing

Al-Taqwa and its Effects - *Shaykh* Rabī' al- Madkhalī

Diseases of the Hearts and Their Cures – *Shaykh* al-Islām Ibn Taymiyyah

Fortress of the Muslims - Invocations from the *Qur'ān* and Sunnah - Darrusalam

The Structure of the Muslim Family - *Shaykh* Muḥammad Amān al-Jāmī

My Sincere Advice to the Women - Umm Abdillah al Wadi'iyyah
Tafsir al- Saʿdī - Parts 28-29-30 - Darrusalam
Authentic Tafsir - Abdulilah Lahmami
The Perfume Seller and the Blacksmith - Concise Words on Good and Bad Companionship - Salafi Publications
Causes Behind the Increase and Decrease of Eemaan - *Shaykh* ʿAbdur-Razzāq al-ʿAbbād
The Correct Creed that Every Muslim Must Know - *Shaykh* ʿAbd al-Salām Ibn Burjiss
The Sealed Nectar- (Biography of the life of Prophet Muḥammad) - Darrusalam
The Stories of the Prophets - *Shaykh* ʿAbd al-Raḥmān al-Saʿdī - Hikmah Publications
Ten Principles in Purification of the Soul - *Shaykh* ʿAbdur-Razzāq al-ʿAbbād - Hikmah Publications

Chapter Thirty-Seven
Glossary of Frequently Used Arabic and Islāmic Terms

The following are frequently used Islāmic and Arabic terms:

Abāyah- the woman's overgarment that extends from the head to the feet
Afwan-You're welcome/excuse me/pardon me
Ahk/Ikhwān/Ikhwa- Brother/brothers
Ahkuuwwa-Islāmic Brotherhood
Ahlul Bida'-The people of innovation
Ahlus Sunnah-the people who practice and hold fast to the Sunnah
Alḥamdulilāh- All praises belong to Allāh; also a person says this after they sneeze
Ālim/Ulamāh- Scholar/Scholars
Allāhumma Bārik- May Allāh make (it) blessed- (Said when you hear of a blessing bestowed on someone)
'Aqīdah-A belief system
Atbā' al Tābi'īn- Generation of Muslims who came after the generation of the *Tābi'īn* and took knowledge from them
Athān- The call to prayer
Aūdhu Billāh- Allāh's refuge/protection is sought
Āyah/Āyāt-Qur'anic verse/verses
BārakAllāhu Feek- May Allāh bless you. Response is usually "*Wa Feek*" (and you).
Bāṭil- Falsehood
Bayt-House
Bi idhnillāh- If Allāh permits/allows
Bida'-innovation
Da'īf- Weak/inauthentic (said of a *Ḥadith*)

Dars/Durūs- Lesson/lessons
Da'wah-Call or invitation to Islām
Dhikr-sayings of invocation and remembrance
Dīn- Religion
Eid al Aḍḥā- The Islāmic holiday that occurs during the season of *Ḥajj* (The 10th day of the twelfth Islāmic month)
Eid al Fitr- The Islāmic holiday that follows the fast of Ramadan (The 1st day of the tenth Islāmic month)
Fatwā/Fatāwā- Religious verdict(s).
Fiqh-Islāmic jurisprudence/understanding
Fiṭrah- the Natural disposition that one is born upon
Ghulū-Extremism
Ḥadith/Aḥādīth- Sayings, actions, approvals, and physical and moral descriptions of Prophet Muḥammad (صَلَّىٱللَّهُعَلَيْهِوَسَلَّمَ)
Ḥafidahullāh- May Allāh preserve him
Ḥalāl-lawful
Ḥamām-Bathroom
Ḥaqq- Truth
Ḥarām-impermissible/unlawful
Hijrah- migration from the land of shirk to the land of Islām
Ibādah-Worship, worship of Allāh
Ifṭār- the act of breaking the fast at sunset/ sometimes used to mean a gathering for the breaking of the fast
In Shā Allāh- If Allāh wills
Iqāmah-The words said after the *athān* and before the prayer begins
Izār- Garment worn by Muslim men on lower half of body that wraps around the waist.
Jāhil/Juhāl-Ignorant (lack or absence of religious knowledge)
Jāhilliyyah- The times of pre-Islāmic ignorance
Janāzah-funeral
Jannah-Paradise

JazākAllāhu Khyran- May Allāh reward you. Response is usually "*Wa Iyyak*" (and you).
Kāfir/Kuffār- Disbeliever/disbelievers
Kayfa Ḥāluka?- How are you. Response can be simply *Alḥamdulilāh, Wa Anta*? All praises are for Allāh, and you? (for men)
Kayfa Ḥāluki?- How are you. Response can be simply Alḥamdulilāh, *Wa Anti*? All praises are for Allāh, and you? (for women)
Khimār- woman's headscarf
Khutbah- religious talk/sermon
Kitāb/Kutub- Book/books
Kūfi- cotton cap worn by Muslim men
Kufr- disbelief
Lā-No
Mā Shā Allāh- Whatever Allāh wills- (Sometimes said in recognition of something good)
Mahr-Dowry (i.e. bridal gift for the woman at marriage)
Makrūh-Disliked (if one leaves it they are rewarded but are not punished if they do it)
Manhaj-A way or methodology
Masjid/Masājid- Mosque/mosques
Mu'min- a believer (one who has *īmān*)
Munkar-an evil matter
Muṣallā-Place of prayer
Musḥaf-All Arabic Qur'ān
Mustaḥabb- an act which is recommended; an act if done one is rewarded but not punished if left off.
Na'm-Yes
Nār-Hellfire
Nikāh-Marriage ceremony
Niqāb- the woman's face veil

Niyyah-intention
Qaddar Allāh- It is what Allāh decreed
Qiblah-Prayer direction
Radiyallāhu Anhu- May Allāh be pleased with him
Radiyallāhu Anhā- May Allāh be pleased with her
Raḥimahullāh- May Allāh have mercy upon him
Ṣabr- Patience
Ṣadaqah-Charity (more general than *Zakāt*).
Ṣaḥābah- Those who met the Prophet believing in him and died upon Islām
Ṣaḥīḥ-authentic such as a hadith. Also can mean right or correct.
Salafiyyah-the practice of the way of the *Salaf*
Shaykh/Mashāyikh- scholar/scholars
Shirk-Association of partners with Allāh in worship
Shukran-Thank you
Suḥūr- the recommended act of eating before the fast starts in Ramadan
Sunnah-Islāmically legislated practices traced back to Prophet Muḥammad (صَلَّىٰٱللَّهُعَلَيْهِوَسَلَّمَ) or his four rightly guided companions
Sūrah -Chapter of the Qur'an
Tābi'īn- Generation of Muslims who came after the *Ṣaḥābah* and took knowledge from them
Tafsīr- Explanation of the Qur'an
Taqwā-Acting in obedience to Allāh and leaving off what He forbade/fear of Allāh.
Taubah- Repentance
Tawḥīd -To single Allāh out with all worship/Allāh's Oneness
Ṭayyib- a good matter/to say ok as an affirmation
Thobe/Thiyāb- Long robe garment wore by Muslim men.
Ukht/Ahkawāt- Sister/sisters
Ummah- Nation
Umrah-A visit performed to Makkah for particular spiritual rituals; it is called the lesser Hajj

Usūl-the core fundamentals of the religion
Wakīl-the one given authority to be the legal Islāmic guardian of a woman
Walīmah-the wedding feast
Walī-the legal Islāmic guardian of a woman from her agnate relatives
Yarḥamukullāh- May Allāh have mercy upon you. Said in reply to the Muslim who sneezes and praises Allāh.
Zawāj- Marriage
Zawjah-Wife
Zawj-Husband

Conclusion

Anything that has been mentioned in this packet which is correct then it is from Allāh and His favor, and whatever it contains which is incorrect, it is from myself and the *shayṭān* [devil], and I seek Allāh's forgiveness from it.

Abū Suhayl Anwar Wright
June 20, 2018
6 *Shawwāl* 1439
Philadelphia, PA

وصلى الله و سلم وبارك على نبينا محمد وعلى آله وصحبه وسلم

May Allāh confer His peace and blessings upon our beloved Prophet Muḥammad, his family and his noble Companions.

Glossary

A

Āyah: (pl. *āyāt*) "sign," a verse of the *Qur'ān*.
Āhād: a narration which has not reached the level of *mutawātir*.
Ahādīth: see *hadīth*.
'Alayhis-salām: "may Allāh (سُبْحَانَهُ وَتَعَالَىٰ) protect and preserve him." It is said after the name of a Prophet of Allāh or after the name of an Angel.
Anṣār: "helpers;" the Muslims of al-Madīnah who supported the Muslims who migrated from Makkah.
'Arsh: Throne of Allāh (جَلَّ جَلَالُهُ).
'Aṣr: the afternoon Prayer.
Awliyā': see *Walī*.

B

Bid'ah: Heresy (any innovatory practice).
Burāq: An animal bigger than a donkey and smaller than a horse on which the Prophet (صَلَّى ٱللَّهُ عَلَيْهِ وَعَلَىٰ آلِهِ وَسَلَّمَ) went for the *Mi'rāj*.

D

Dā'ī: one engaged in *da'wah*, caller.
Da'aef: "weak," unauthentic narration.
Da'wah: invitation, call to Allāh (عَزَّ وَجَلَّ).
Dīn: a completed way of life prescribed by Allāh (تَبَارَكَ وَتَعَالَىٰ).
Dhikr: (pl. *adhkār*) remembrance of Allāh (جَلَّ وَعَلَا) with the heart, sayings of the tongue and actions of our limbs.

E

Īmān: faith, to affirm all that was revealed to the Prophet (صَلَّى ٱللَّهُ عَلَيْهِ وَسَلَّمَ).

F

Fāhish: one who uses foul language.
Fard Kifāyah: collective obligation - if fulfilled by a part of the community then the rest are not obligated.
Fatwā: (pl. *fatāwā*) religious verdicts.
Faqīh: A scholar who can give religious verdicts.
Fiqh: Islāmic jurisprudence, understanding.
Fitnah: (pl. *fitan*) Trials, persecution, conflicts and strifes.
Fitrah: the natural disposition that one is born upon.

G

Ghulū: going to an extreme.
Ghusl: A ceremonial bath necessary for the one who is in a state of *Janābah*.

H

Hadīth: (pl. *ahādīh*) the saying, actions and approvals narrated from the Prophet (صَلَّى ٱللَّهُ عَلَيْهِ وَعَلَىٰ آلِهِ وَسَلَّمَ).
Halāl: lawful.
Hanīf: pure Islāmic Monotheism (worshipping Allāh alone and nothing else).

Harām: unlawful and forbidden.
Hasan: fine, good; a term used for an authentic *hadīth*, which does not reach the level of *Sahīh*.
Harj: killing.
Al-Harūriyyah: an especially un-orthodox religious sect that branched off from the *Khawārij*.
Hijrahh: migration from the land of *Shirk* to the land of Islām.
Hukm: a judgment of legal decision (especially of Allāh).

I

'Ibādah: worship, worship of Allāh.
Ihsān: worshipping Allāh as though you see Him. However, since you cannot see Him, then know that He sees you.
Ijmā': consensus, a unified opinion of Scholars regarding a certain issue.
Ijtihād: exertion of effort; the process of arriving at a reasoned decision by a Scholar on an issue.
Imām: leaders; leaders in Prayer, knowledge in *fiqh*, leader of a state.
Isnād: the chain of narrators linking the collector of the saying to the person quoted.
Istikhārah: a Prayer consisting of two units (*rak'ah*) asking Allāh for guidance.
Istiwā: ascending; the ascending of Allāh above the Throne (in the manner that befits His Majesty).

J

Janābah: state of a person after having sexual intercourse or sexual discharge.
Janāzah: (pl. *janā'iz*): Funeral.

Jihād: striving, struggling, fighting to make the Word of Allāh supreme.
Jumʿah: Friday.
Jinn: invisible creation, created by Allāh from smokeless fire.
Junub: a person who is in the state of *janābah*.

K

Kaʿbah: a square stone building in *al-Masjidul-Haram* (the great mosque in Makkah which Muslims go to for pilgrimage and which all Muslims direct their face in Prayer).
Al-Kabāʾir: the major sins.
Khārijī: (pl. *Khawārij*): those who declared that a Muslim becomes a disbeliever due to committing a major sin alone.
Khalīfah: (pl. *khulafāʾ*): the head of the Islāmic government to whom the oath of allegiance is given.
Khilāfah: an Islāmic state.
Khutbah: (person *khatīb)*, religious talk (sermon).
Kufr: (person *kāfir*) act of disbelief in the Religion of Islām.

M

Madhhab: position or opinion of a Scholar; school of Islāmic Jurisprudence.
Makrūh: not approved of, undesirable from the point of view of Religion, although not punʿIshāble.
Manhaj: way; method; methodology.
Marfūʿ: raised; a narration attributed to the Prophet (صَلَّىٰٱللَّهُعَلَيْهِوَسَلَّمَ).
Masjid: mosque.
Mawbiqāt: great destructive sins.
Mudallis: one who practises *tadlīs*.

Muhājir: (pl. *muhājirūn, muhājirīn*) one who migrated from the land of the disbelievers to the land of the Muslims for the sake of Allāh.
Muhaddith: scholar of the science of *hadīth*.
Muftī: one who gives *fatāwā*.
Mujāhid: (pl. *mujāhidūn*): a Muslim warrior in *Jihād*.
Mujtahid: one who is qualified to pass judgment using *ijtihād*.
Munkar: "rejected;" a narration which is un-authentic itself and contradicts and authentic narrations.
Muqallid: one who practices *taqlīd*.
Mushrik: (pl. *mushrikūn*) polytheists, pagans and disbelievers in the oneness of Allāh (عَزَّوَجَلَّ) and His Messenger (صَلَّىٰ اللَّهُ عَلَيْهِ وَعَلَىٰ آلِهِ وَسَلَّمَ).
Mustahabb: recommended; an action if left it is not punishable and if done it is rewardable.
Muttaqūn: those who are pious.
Mutawātir: a *hadīth* which is narrated by a very large number of narrators, such that it cannot be supported that they all agreed upon a lie.
Muwahhid: (pl. *muwahhidūn*) one who unifies all of his worship and directs it to Allāh alone.
Mawdū': fabricated; spurious; invented (narration).
Mawqūf: stopped; a narration from a Companion (not going back to the Prophet (صَلَّىٰ اللَّهُ عَلَيْهِ وَسَلَّمَ)).
Mawsūl: "connected;" a continuous *isnād* (can be narrated back to the Prophet (صَلَّىٰ اللَّهُ عَلَيْهِ وَسَلَّمَ)).

N

Nāfilah: (pl. *nawāfil*) Optional practice of worship.
Niyyah: intention from the heart.
Nusuk: a sacrifice.

Q

Qadar: Divine pre-ordainment; that which Allāh has ordained for his creation.
Qiblah: the direction the Muslims face during Prayer.
Qiyās: analogical deduction of Islāmic laws. New laws are deduced from old laws based upon similarity between their causes.
Qunūt: "devotion;" a special supplication while standing in the Prayer.
Quraysh: one of the greatest tribes in Arabia in the pre-Islāmic period of Ignorance. The Prophet (صَلَّى ٱللَّهُ عَلَيْهِ وَسَلَّمَ) belonged to this tribe.

R

Rāfidī: the correct title for the extreme *Shī'ah.* Those who bear malice and grudges against the noble Companions (رَضِيَ ٱللَّهُ عَنْهُمْ) to the extent that they declare them to be apostates. They also hold that the *Qur'ān* which the Muslims have is neither complete nor preserved from corruption.
Ramadān: the ninth month of Islāmic calendar, in which Muslims observe fasting.

S

Sahābah: Muslims who met the Prophet (صَلَّى ٱللَّهُ عَلَيْهِ وَسَلَّمَ) believing in him and died believing in him.
Sahīh: authentic, the highest rank of classification of authentic *ahādīth.*
Salaf/Salafus-Sālihīn: pious predecessors; the Muslims of the first three generations: the Companions, the successors and their successors.
Salafī: one who ascribes oneself to the *salaf* and follows their way.
Sīrah: the life story of the Prophet (صَلَّى ٱللَّهُ عَلَيْهِ وَعَلَىٰ آلِهِ وَسَلَّمَ).

Sharī'ah: the divine code of law of Islām.
Shawwāl: the month after *Ramadān.*
Shaytān: Satan
Shī'ah: (see *Rāfidī*) a collective name for various sects claiming love for *Ahlul-Bayt.*
Shirk: associating partners with Allāh directly or indirectly; compromising any aspects of *Tawhīd.*
Sūrah: a chapter of the *Qur'ān*
Sunnah: "example, practice;" the way of life of the Prophet (صَلَّى اللَّهُ عَلَيْهِ وَسَلَّمَ), consisting of his words, actions and silent approvals. The *Sunnah* is contained in various *ahādīth.*

T

Tābi'ī: (pl. *tābi'īn*) the generation that came after the Companions of the Prophet (صَلَّى اللَّهُ عَلَيْهِ وَسَلَّمَ).
Tafsīr: explanation of the *Qur'ān.*
Tāghūt: anything worshiped other than the real God (Allāh) (i.e. false deities).
Tahajjud: voluntary, recommended Prayer between the compulsory prayers of *'Ishā'* and *Fajr.*
Takhrīj: to reference a *hadīth* to its sources and analyze its *isnads.*
Taqlīd: blind following; to follow someone's opinion (*madhhab*) without evidence.
Taqwā: acting in obedience to Allāh, hoping for His mercy upon light from Him and *taqwā* is leaving acts of disobedience, out of fear of Him, upon light from Him.
Tarjamah: notes about a reporter of *hadīth.*
Tawwāf: the circumambulation of the *Ka'bah.*
Tawhīd: Islāmic Monotheism. The Oneness of Allāh. Believing and acting upon His Lordship, His rights of Worship and Names and Attributes.

U

Uhud: A well known mountain in al-Madīnah. One of the greatest battles in Islāmic history came at its foot. This is called *Ghazwah Uhud.*
'Ulamā': (singular: *'ālim*) scholars.
Umm: mother of, used as an identification.
Ummah [nation]: "nation", the Muslims as a whole.
'Umrah: a visit to Makkah during which one performs the *tawwāf* around the *Ka'bah* and the *Sa'ī* between *as-Safā* and *al-Marwah.* It is called the lesser *Hajj.*
Usūl: the fundamentals.

W

Wahyī: the revelation or inspiration of Allāh to His Prophets.
Wahdatul-Wujūd: the belief that everything in existence is infact Allāh. This deviant belief is held by many *Sūfīs.*
Wakīl: disposer of affairs.
Witr: "odd;" the last Prayer at the night, which consists of odd number of *raka'āt* (units).
Walīmah: the wedding feast.
Wasīlah: the means of approach or achieving His closeness to Allāh by getting His favours.
Wudū': an ablution (ritual washing) that is performed before Prayer and other kinds of worship.

Y

Yaqīn: perfect absolute faith.
Yathrib: one of the names of al-Madīnah.

Z

Zakāt: charity that is obligatory on everyone who has wealth over and above a certain limit over which a year has passed (2.5% of saved wealth).

Zakātul-Fitr: an obligatory charity by the Muslims to be given to the poor before the Prayer of *'Īdul-Fitr.*

Zamzam: the sacred water inside the *haram* (the grand mosque) at Makkah.

Zanādiqah: atheists, heretics.

Our Call to the Ummah

[1]: We believe in Allāh and His Names and Attributes, as they were mentioned in the Book of Allāh and in the *Sunnah* of the Messenger of Allāh (عَزَّوَجَلَّ), without *taḥrīf* (distortion), nor *ta'wīl* (figurative interpretation), nor *tamthīl* (making a likeness), nor *tashbīh* (resemblance), nor *ta'ṭīl* (denial).

[2]: We love the Companions (رَضِيَٱللَّهُعَنْهُمْ) of the Messenger of Allaah (صَلَّىٱللَّهُعَلَيْهِوَسَلَّمَ), and we hate those who speak against them. We believe that to speak ill of them is to speak ill of the Religion, because they are the ones who conveyed it to us. And we love the Family of the Prophet (صَلَّىٱللَّهُعَلَيْهِوَسَلَّمَ) with love that is permitted by the *Sharī'ah*.

[3]: We love the People of *Ḥadīth* and all of the *Salaf* of the *Ummah* from *Ahl al-Sunnah*. Imām al-Shāṭibī (d.790H) - رَحِمَهُٱللَّهُ - said, "The *Salaf al-Ṣāliḥ*, the Companions, the *tābi'īn* and their successors knew the *Qur'ān*, its sciences and its meanings the best."

[4]: We despise *'ilm al-kalām* (knowledge of theological rhetoric), and we view it to be from amongst the greatest reasons for the division in the *Ummah*.

[5]: We do not accept anything from the books of *fiqh* (jurisprudence), nor from the books of *tafsīr* (explanation of the *Qur'ān*), nor from the ancient stories, nor from the *Sīrah* (biography) of the Prophet (صَلَّىٱللَّهُعَلَيْهِوَسَلَّمَ), except that which has been confirmed from Allāh or from His Messenger

(صَلَّى ٱللَّهُ عَلَيْهِ وَسَلَّمَ). We do not mean that we have rejected them, nor do we claim that we are not in need of them. Rather, we benefit from the discoveries of our Scholars and the jurists and other than them. However, we do not accept a ruling, except with an authentic proof.

[6]: We do not write in our books, nor do we cover in our lessons, nor do we give sermons with anything except the *Qur'ān*, or the authentic and authoritative *ḥadīth.* And we detest what emanates from many books and admonishers in terms of false stories and weak and fabricated *aḥādīth.*

[7]: We do not perform *takfīr* upon any Muslim due to any sin, except *Shirk* with Allāh, or the abandonment of Prayer, or apostasy. We seek refuge in Allāh from that.

[8]: We believe that the *Qur'ān* is the Speech of Allāh, it is not created.

[9]: We hold that our 'obligation is to co-operate with the group that traverses the methodology of the Book and the *Sunnah*, and what the *Salaf* of the *Ummah* were upon; in terms of calling to Allāh (سُبْحَانَهُ وَتَعَالَىٰ), and being sincere in worship of Him, and warning from *Shirk*, innovations, and disobedience, and to advise all of the groups that oppose this.' 'So co-operating upon righteousness and piety (*taqwā*) and mutual advising necessitates warning against evil and not co-operating with the wicked.'

[10]: We do not deem it correct to revolt against the Muslim rulers as long as they are Muslims, nor do we feel that revolutions bring about reconciliation. Rather, they corrupt the community.

[11]: We hold that this multiplicity of present day parties is a reason for the division of the Muslims and their weakness. So therefore we set about 'freeing the minds from the fetters of blind-following and the darkness of sectarianism and party spirit.'

[12]: We restrict our understanding of the Book of Allāh and of the *Sunnah* of the Messenger of Allāh (صَلَّى ٱللَّهُ عَلَيْهِ وَسَلَّمَ) to the understanding of the *Salaf* of the *Ummah* from the Scholars of *ḥadīth*, not the blind-followers of their individuals. Rather, we take the truth from wherever it comes. And we know that there are those who claim *Salafīyah*, yet *Salafīyah* is free from them, since they bring to the society what Allāh has prohibited. We believe in 'cultivating the young generation upon this Islām, purified from all that we have mentioned, giving to them a correct Islamic education from the start - without any influence from the disbelieving western education.'

[13]: We believe that politics is a part of the Religion, and those who try to separate the Religion from politics are only attempting to destroy the Religion and to spread chaos.

[14]: We believe there will be no honor or victory for the Muslims until they return to the Book of Allāh and to the *Sunnah* of the Messenger of Allāh (صَلَّى ٱللَّهُ عَلَيْهِ وَسَلَّمَ).

[15]: We oppose those who divide the Religion into trivialities and important issues. And we know that this is a destructive *Daʿwah*.

[16]: We oppose those who put down the knowledge of the *Sunnah*, and say that this is not the time for it. Likewise, we oppose those who put down acting upon the *Sunnah* of the Messenger of Allāh (صَلَّى ٱللَّهُ عَلَيْهِ وَسَلَّمَ).

[17]: Our *Daʿwah* and our *ʿAqīdah* is more beloved to us than our own selves, our wealth and our offspring. So we are not prepared to part with it for gold, nor silver. We say this so that no one may have hope in buying out our *Daʿwah*, nor should he think that it is possible for him to purchase it from us for *dīnār* or *dirham*.

[18]: We love the present day Scholars of the *Sunnah* and hope to benefit from them and regret the passing away of many of them. Imām Mālik said (d.179H) - رَحِمَهُ ٱللَّهُ, "The knowledge of *ḥadīth* is your flesh and blood and you will be asked concerning it on the Day of Judgment, so look who you are taking it from."

[19]: We do not accept a *fatwā* except from the Book of Allāh and the *Sunnah* of the Messenger of Allāh (صَلَّى ٱللَّهُ عَلَيْهِ وَسَلَّمَ).

These are glimpses into our *'Aqīdah* and our *Da'wah*. So if one has any objection to this, then we are prepared to accept advice if it is truthful, and to refute it if it is erroneous, and to avoid it if it is stubborn rejection. And Allāh knows best.

Notes

Notes

Notes

Notes

Notes

Notes

Notes

Notes